Secrets of a

Secrets of a
Buccaneer-Scholar

*How Self-Education and the Pursuit of Passion
Can Lead to a Lifetime of Success*

JAMES MARCUS BACH

SIMON &
SCHUSTER

London · New York · Sydney · Toronto

A CBS COMPANY

First published in Great Britain in 2009 by Simon & Schuster UK Ltd
A CBS COMPANY

Original art by Mary Alton

1 3 5 7 9 10 8 6 4 2

Simon & Schuster UK Ltd
1st Floor
222 Gray's Inn Road
London
WC1X 8HB

www.simonandschuster.co.uk

Simon & Schuster Australia
Sydney

A CIP catalogue copy for this book is available
from the British Library.

ISBN: 978-1-84737-535-3

Designed by Carla Jayne Jones

Printed in the UK by CPI Mackays, Chatham ME5 8TD

To my father, Richard Bach, a Cheshire Cat in a flight suit.
He appears at every crossroad of my life, and always smiling.

Contents

Contents

Contents

Secrets of a
Buccaneer-Scholar

1

Dangerous Ideas

Schoolteachers don't like me very much

Years ago I was invited to speak at a special school for "at risk" kids. These kids had quit or been thrown out of normal high school. I was twenty-four, and working as a software test manager at Apple Computer in Silicon Valley. The kids' teacher had heard about me. Since I was a high school dropout who "made good," she asked me to explain the importance of a good education to her students. I wanted to bring an encouraging message. This is what I told them:

> Education is important. School is not. I didn't need school. Neither do you.
>
> School can help your education. Maybe you like school. If it's fun, stay with it.

If you're not happy, leave this place. If you think there's no other way to get your education, or if you think you can't get a good job without this place, then look at me.

I am proof that there is another way to do it.

I left high school because it wasn't helping me. I felt that I was wasting my time. So, I developed my own approach to learning. I taught myself computer programming. Now I'm twenty-four. I've been a manager in research and development at Apple Computer for the last four years. They hired me because I showed them I could do the work, even though I had no degree.

Education is vital to the work I do and the life I want to build. I study almost every day in the coffee shop next door to my office. I study software engineering, systems thinking, philosophy, and history—whatever my heart wants to study.

I study, but I don't go to school.

School is temporary. Education is not. If you want to prosper in life: find something that fascinates you and jump all over it. Don't wait for someone to teach you; your enthusiasm will attract teachers to you. Don't worry about diplomas or degrees; just get so good that no one can ignore you.

The students seemed surprised to hear this. They had questions:

How did you get Apple to hire you without a degree?
I knew how to program computers because I taught myself by reading and studying the technical manuals. I wrote video games professionally after I left school, and there was one manager at Apple who liked my experience and enthusiasm. After that, I just showed I could learn fast and do good work.

But how did you even get an interview with them?
I wrote a résumé listing my experiences and projects. It looked pretty good. I sent it to a contracting agency. They sent it to Apple.

Isn't it true that many employers won't even consider you unless you have lots of formal education?
Maybe it's true. So what? I'm not trying to get a job with *many* employers. One at a time is good enough. There are always *some* who value what is truly useful, such as technical skill and the ability to play well with others. Find those people.

Why did you leave school in the first place?
I believed it was interfering with my education. I felt that it wasn't just a waste of my time—it was using my own time against me. I needed to build confidence and independence, and school was tearing me down. Schools are good for some people, and I bet, somewhere, there are schools that would have been good for me. I never found one, so I took matters into my own hands. In that process I discovered that education is so much more than school.

Are you saying we don't really have to do homework?
Only you can answer that for yourself. Me? I rarely did schoolwork that followed me home. I'll tell you this, though: If you want to take control of your life with the power of your mind, then you'll be doing "homework" whether or not you go to school.

What if I'm not interested in anything? What if I'm lazy?
If you were very hungry, would you make the effort to eat, or would you be lazy and starve? I don't believe in lazy. You just need to find what you're hungry for. So, get out and try different things. One way to try different things is to go to school. Another way is to leave school. Or you can do some of both.

Doesn't learning require discipline and hard work? (The teacher asked this from the back of the room.)
To learn something valuable, you may have to work at it. It may be *hard* work. For me, it has to be fun, too. Or else forget it. The secret to my success is this: I found something that was fun for me, I learned all about it, and now I get paid for fun things I do with my mind.

After the Lecture . . .

I felt good after talking to the class. I liked the idea of working with kids. People have helped me along the way. I wanted to return the favor. As I was leaving, the teacher joined me.

"Mr. Bach, I want you to know that I will recommend against you speaking at our school again," she said. "Your message is dangerous for children to hear."

She was almost right. It was dangerous, what I said—dangerous for *her.* To maintain a docile herd of students, her school needs them to accept certain truths:

- You *must* study what we tell you. What we say is the *only* thing that matters.
- You *must* pass our tests. Our tests measure the *only* important things about you.
- You *must* attend school. *Only* through schooling can you hope to enjoy a good life.

This is what I call *schoolism*—the belief that schooling is the necessary and exclusive way to get a good education. *Must* and *only!*

"I told them about myself," I said, "and how I came to be here. I told them the truth."

"It may be true for *you,*" she replied. "But these kids aren't super smart like you. They don't come from well-off families. They're barely staying in school, and you just told them that they don't need to be here. They *do* need to be here!"

"Ma'am, my eighth-grade English teacher told me I would have to pump gas for a living if I didn't graduate high school. She was wrong about my future. Isn't it possible your students will surprise you, too? I think any of your students can do what I did—in high tech, journalism, business, art, or any number of different fields. And they have a lifetime to develop their talents. What's the rush?"

"Yes they could be successful if they put in the work," she conceded. "But I don't think they heard that part of your message. I'm barely holding on to some of these kids as it is. I'm afraid you've made my job much harder, Mr. Bach. Some of them are going to take a 'what the hell' attitude instead of applying themselves."

"So what if they do?" I replied. "This is America. They probably won't starve. They probably won't be eaten by wolves. If they don't care about education, they may be forced to work at low-skilled jobs they won't enjoy, such as fast food or house cleaning. However bad those fates may sound, they are neither fatal nor permanent. Or perhaps they will accidentally educate themselves by starting a new business, building things, or doing theatre, music, or sports. Are you worried they'll turn to crime? Then show them *more* options, not fewer. They will learn and grow from anything that happens, *unless they believe there is no hope.* Your job is not to make them huddle quietly in a corral, but to help them get out there and seek their fortunes. Show them a way!"

I had to shrug about this as I drove back to work. I'm no political activist. I can never convince the bureaucrats to abandon their mythology of social order. I think very differently than most people about social order. I'm a buccaneer.

But I'm not talking to bureaucrats. I'm talking to you.

THIS BOOK IS NOT ABOUT SCHOOL

I don't care about school. I care about living and prospering as a free thinker. I want you to be free, too. In this book, I share stories about school in order to highlight the differences between self-education and institutional education. I will describe what we're up against and why I had to find another way.

I will share my own experiences. But none of this is about me alone. It's about an approach to intellectual life that is open to all of us. Join me in exploring it.

What Is Education?

Education is not a heap of facts. It's not the hours we spend in classrooms, or the way we answer test questions. It's not indoctrination, nor worshipping the ancients, nor obedience to authority, not taking anyone's word for what is true, false, vital, banal.

Education is the "you" that emerges from the learning you do.

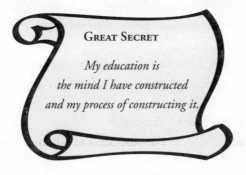

GREAT SECRET

*My education is
the mind I have constructed
and my process of constructing it.*

Everyone in the world, then, is *already educated* in some way. We humans construct our minds, deconstruct them, then reconstruct them throughout our lives. You are doing it right now, as you read. You are wondering, "What does he mean when he says that?"; and perhaps when you read the words "construct" and "deconstruct" you saw images in your mind of lumber, steel beams, machinery, and chaos. Those pictures in your head are part of the puzzle-solving, model-making process that is self-construction. If there comes a moment when the pictures and ideas make sense to you and you feel "oh, *that's* how it works," a new addition to yourself has been constructed.

Knowledge is part of my education only if it changes me. Knowledge does not improve my education unless it changes me for the better. It might make me more powerful, more insightful, more engaged with life. But I must become more *interesting or useful* to myself in some way, or there's no improvement.

No one on earth has a choice about whether or not to be educated. But we do have a choice about what form that education will take. It's a life's work.

Other people may help me, even institutions. But my education belongs only to me, as yours belongs to you.

This book is about how I developed my own education on my own terms, how that unorthodox education brought me success, and how you, too, can do it your way.

2

I Am a Buccaneer-Scholar

What's that and so what?

I am a thinker with the temperament of a buccaneer.

A buccaneer-scholar is *anyone whose love of learning is not muzzled, yoked, or shackled by any institution or authority; whose mind is driven to wander and find its own voice and place in the world.*

For two decades, this has been the way I understand myself. I use the metaphor of buccaneering not just for learning but also to deal with the emotional battles within myself and the intellectual battles I sometimes fight with other people. It helps me feel better about being an outsider. Whenever I meet people who think for themselves, I see them as fellow buccaneers.

Can you be a buccaneer and take advice and direction from a teacher you respect? Of course. If you listen to a teacher because that's your pleasure, and not just because you feel trapped, then you may be a buccaneer. If you feel free to disagree with your teachers, take some things from them and ignore other things, you may be a buccaneer.

I'm self-educated, yet I have had many mentors and fellow students who helped me grow. I'm grateful to them. I claim my independence, but I also feel part of a larger mind that includes other thinkers. I feel complete in myself *and* part of a community, too.

Even people who live radical and independent must come to terms with the rest of the world. I have done that. I have my strange ideas and home-brew study methods, yet I can still please employers, attract clients, listen, and learn from other minds.

MY PAPER CREDENTIALS

I am a certified graduate of the eighth grade. This is the only diploma-like document I possess. I refused to do a lot of my schoolwork, and

I intentionally failed some tests. Nevertheless, the Vermont State Board of Education claimed that I graduated.

HIGH SCHOOL DROPOUT

As you can see, I dropped out of high school.

My transcript may look a bit strange.

I liked math. My mother talked the school into letting me take geometry and trigonometry in ninth grade. I didn't receive grades for these classes, though, because instead of taking the final exams, I went to the University of Vermont to take a summer calculus course.

Name of
Student................... Bach, James ....

STUDENT ACADEMIC PERMANENT RECORD

1980-81 Gr. 9	FM	CR	R
English	78	1	
Social Studies	84	1	
Physical Science	94	1	
Math 10			
Math 11			
French	70	1	
Physical Education	85	¼	

1981-82 Grade 10	FM	CR	R
English	63		
Social Studies	83	1	
Calculus II	83	1	
Physics	49		
Math 10	91	1	88
Math 11	81	1	72
Physical Ed.	87	¼	

My ninth-grade math teacher was furious that I missed his exams. I couldn't take him seriously. The point is learning, right? Not grades. By that time I had contempt for grades. To me, the public school grading system seemed fraudulent and ignorant. I felt this way because I often received good grades I knew I hadn't earned, while some of my worst grades were for subjects in which I excelled.

See that *94* in ninth-grade science? I barely attended that class. Most days, I skipped it and played in the computer lab instead. I went to science class each Friday to take the test, which was a weak mix of vocabulary words and multiple-choice questions about basic facts of nature. Even though I turned in no homework, passing such tests was apparently enough to get a good grade.

See that *49* in tenth-grade physics? Looks like a low score, doesn't it? But I loved physics. I studied it at home. I made drawings of spaceships and calculated how fast they could go and how long it would take them to reach Alpha Centauri. I taught myself to use a sliderule and calculated trajectories of rockets that put space stations into orbit, the centrifugal forces on those space stations, and the energy of meteoroids that might strike them in orbit.

But none of that was part of my schoolwork. So it didn't count. Instead, physics in my school was a process designed to minimize the probability that any student would fail physics class. This was accomplished by emptying physics of much of its content. The subject was changed from an exploration of the patterns of the universe into a ritual of simple observations and simple calculations.

The problem was the labs. We were supposed to do them each week. A "lab" was a set of instructions in a book and blanks to fill in.

These were turned in to the teacher, so that he could check that the blanks were filled with the expected numbers.

Example: "The ball rolled 1 meter in _____ seconds when released on the 10 degree plane."

These labs were represented to us as "experiments," but there was no inquiry in them. They were just rituals for getting a grade. In practice, a few students performed the ritual to obtain the magic numbers; the rest copied the numbers into their own workbooks.

For me, the labs turned physics into a sham. I was told I would not pass the class unless I turned in my completed workbook. Instead, I turned in nothing. My workbook remained empty the whole year, I failed physics, but to this day I feel good that I took a stand for ethics in education.

At the end of tenth grade, a year after I skipped the math exams, my geometry and trigonometry teacher suddenly reappeared. The man was *still angry with me for missing his pointless tests*. He forced me to go into a room where the same exams were being held and said I had to take them. I didn't care about the grade, but math is fun, so I went along. That's why my Math 10 and Math 11 scores show up in tenth grade instead of ninth.

So you see. There are a lot of numbers on my high school transcript. The numbers look plain and clear, but the story behind them is nothing of the kind. Schools can't track or describe students like me in meaningful terms. High numbers don't represent good learning; low numbers don't represent bad. The result is a nonsensical record from which little of value can be inferred.

We can't know from looking at any report card or transcript how well or poorly a student is doing at school. These records don't even tell us how well a student "plays the game" of school because a teacher may decide to pass an otherwise failing student for the sake of mercy, decorum, or administrative pressure. The system is a mess.

I have no "General Equivalency Diploma." I have no other college credit. I have no certifications other than a driver's license, a student pilot's license, an open water diver rating, and a Level I paraglider pilot license.

If you measure people by paper credentials, you would be comfortable ignoring me. By that measure, I'm the Invisible Man.

My True Credentials

Google me. You'll find that "James Bach" comes up often in connection with computer software testing.

- As I write this book, I've worked in the computing field for twenty-four years.
- At twenty, I was one of twenty-two group managers in the product quality assurance division of Apple Computer. There were more than four hundred engineers in that division. As far as I knew, I was the youngest manager in the entire company. That was in 1987.
- I've written books and many articles since then about software development and testing.
- I've pioneered new approaches to testing and testing education. In 1999, Microsoft put out a press release that referred to me as a testing expert.

- I've been a keynote speaker at software conferences around the world. I've lectured in Israel, South Korea, Singapore, Australia, New Zealand, Germany, Ireland, Scotland, England, Netherlands, Sweden, Austria, India, Canada, and the United States.
- I've taught at high-profile laboratories such as Los Alamos, Lawrence Livermore, and Jet Propulsion Laboratories. Twice I have made the opening keynote speech at conferences where nearly everyone in the audience held a PhD.
- I've lectured at universities such as the University of Colorado, Florida Tech, and the Milwaukee School of Engineering and served on a National Science Foundation merit review committee. My writings are used in engineering courses in various universities, including Massachusetts Institure of Technology (MIT) and Stanford.
- In 1994, I was on the industrial advisory committee that reviewed the first undergraduate degree in software engineering for the Rochester Institute of Technology.
- I'm one of the few software testers ever mentioned in the *Wall Street Journal.*

I didn't earn these credentials by paying an institution to print my name in calligraphy. I got them by doing meaningful work. My work is discussed in other peoples' books about building software. My writings are on the Web for anyone to evaluate. Other people vouch for me, including a few academics.

For people who live by ideas, as I do, our *reputations* become our credentials. Our ideas make our names. Our names become our brand.

My credentials work. They are specific to me, and allow me to market myself as a unique resource. I have developed my personal brand.

Here's why I succeed:

- I invested time and passion in my own self-education.
- I developed a method of self-education that fits my temperament and the rhythms of my mind.
- I work in a field that values competence and good ideas more than paper credentials.
- I found mentors and colleagues who helped me gain the confidence to present my ideas in a compelling way.

Anyone can do this.

I succeed not because I have powerful friends, or a lot of money, but because I am *better educated* at my craft than many of my competitors. My education is a competitive advantage.

As a buccaneer-scholar, I'm a free thinker and a crafty, passionate learner, whose thoughts are not limited by someone else's curriculum or philosophy.

Today, I sell training and consulting for a living. Just as I don't have traditional credentials, I don't do traditional advertising. I put my ideas on the Web, speak at conferences, and trust that someone will call me with work. It's a word-of-mouth and word-of-Web business. It can be nerve-wracking, hoping that opportunity will knock its way past the spam filters. But for nearly ten years, it has.

I am paid a lot of money when I teach my classes. They are packed with ideas. Where did those ideas come from? They come from the relentless, whimsical, low-intensity learning process I call buccaneering.

3

The First Buccaneers

A free people, skilled in many arts

WHO WERE THE BUCCANEERS?

You might think "buccaneer" is just another word for pirate, but the buccaneers were not necessarily pirates. They didn't say "Arr, Matey!" (that comes from the 1950 movie version of *Treasure Island*). And few wore eye patches, walked planks, or buried treasure.

The first buccaneers were French and English hunters and farmers in the Caribbean who settled on the island of St. Kitts in 1625. They got their name from the way they preserved meat—a process called "boucanning." You'd think that a people named for food preparation would lead exciting lives, but actually, life was rather quiet at first. Not until 1629, when they were nearly exterminated by a Spanish expedition, did the buccaneers begin to write history.

After the Spanish attack, the buccaneers fled to the islands of

Hispaniola and Tortuga. They hatched an idea: "Instead of hunting and farming and drying meat all day, let's rob Spanish ships and villages!" So they began to cruise the surrounding islands and the northern coast of South America (called "the Spanish Main"), looking for booty.

Successful buccaneers would have piles of gold and silver and throw amazing-huge parties. Indeed by all accounts, the way to get rich in the new world was to be a tavern-keeper in Jamaica, since that's where most buccaneers spent their loot before going out once again to hunt the seas.

Even after taking up piracy, they still called themselves buccaneers, which must have been strange for the Spanish, at first:

"Buccaneers are coming!"

"The beef jerky guys? Are you telling me that a band of drunken, sea-roving barbecue chefs is chasing our ship? I don't see the problem. Tell them we've *had* lunch."

You have to understand about the Spanish. Spain had discovered the New World, and they claimed to own everything in it. Pope Alexander VI confirmed this in a papal proclamation (the Pope, as it happened, was Spanish).

Meanwhile, the Reformation was in full force, which meant newly Protestant countries like England and Holland were eager *not* to obey the Pope. As a result, Spain owned the New World the way it might own a broken piñata: candy everywhere, and a lot of kids diving for it.

The strategy of the buccaneers was to wait until a Spanish kid collected a shirt full of candy bars, then jump him as he waddled away.

The seventeenth-century buccaneers were an important force that shaped the development of the New World. Their independence of spirit and the effect they had on the great powers of Europe inspire me as I live and learn today. Here's what you need to know about them:

- They were a skilled, self-reliant community. They were not under the thumb of any government. They were free people, carving their fortunes from a frontier land. They lived in the original "wild west"—the West Indies.
- They were an inclusive transnational and polyglot community: English, French, Portuguese, Basque, Dutch, West Indian, and African.
- Few of them were born in the New World. Men were drawn there from other places by the promise of freedom, wealth, and excitement. Repelled by the smothering civilization of Europe, they *chose* to be buccaneers and paid for that choice.
- They were amphibious—equally at home on land and sea—and multi-skilled. They hunted, planted, built ships, and sailed to battle.
- The buccaneers had no commitments other than those they made to one another. They had no families, no regular jobs, and no need to stay home. They were free to rove.
- They operated without material support. They didn't have dockyards or provisioners. They didn't have insurance. The only people who invested in their cruises were other buccaneers.

- There were never many of them, a few thousand at most. It was a hard life. But by weakening Spain, their success changed the course of history.
- They targeted the Spanish, whose wealth came from brutalizing the indigenous people of the Americas. The seventeenth-century buccaneers were plunderers plundering other plunderers, and that gave them, in their own minds, moral high ground.
- Spain's enemies blessed the buccaneers, who sometimes fought right alongside the royal navies of France and England. In that capacity, they were called *privateers*. In other words, sometimes the buccaneers went corporate.
- They might have become a nation, but drunk and broke from all their partying, they couldn't quite get themselves organized.

WHAT DOES THIS HAVE TO DO WITH EDUCATION?

I'll tell you why I'm drawn to buccaneers: They were bold and aggressive, they lived free, and they lived by their wits. That's how I want to be as a thinker.

"Buccaneering" is a grand metaphor for the way some of us learn. It gives comfort and encouragement to those of us with minds that love to rove, minds that *can't help* roving. Some people call that an "attention deficit" disorder. No, it's more like *unstoppable curiosity*.

I call myself a buccaneer-scholar, and I live in creative tension. The word "scholar" implies someone who is trained by a school or belongs to a school; "buccaneer" evokes relentless *self*-creation. I belong to the school of no schools.

Here is how the buccaneering metaphor works:

- The original buccaneers sailed in ships on the sea. The vehicle used by buccaneer-scholars is their minds, and they sail in the world of ideas.
- Buccaneers embarked on cruises in search of treasure. The cruise of a buccaneer-scholar takes the form of a self-determined curriculum. A buccaneer-scholar embarks on a cruise in search of knowledge.
- Buccaneers used the threat of violence to achieve their ends. Buccaneer-scholars are not physically violent; they are audacious and intellectually passionate. They use irreverent inquiry rather than malevolent artillery to seize the treasure that they seek.
- Buccaneers quested for material wealth, such as gold bullion, jewels, and silver coins called "pieces of eight." The wealth that buccaneer-scholars seek is less tangible but no less valuable: knowledge, skills, great secrets, connections with other minds, and an ever more powerful self.

The buccaneering metaphor is appropriate because both the original buccaneers and modern buccaneer-scholars are potentially dangerous people. The historical buccaneers were physically dangerous. They *harmed* their victims by stealing from them. Buccaneer-scholars are sometimes considered dangerous because their methods and ideas threaten the status quo. Still, ideas are inalienable. They are what economists call "non-rival" goods: if I learn from you, I'm not decreasing what you know. If I study medicine without going to medical school, no doctor is the poorer for it. Intellectual buccaneering can be disruptive, even offensive, but it does no other harm. It preserves the spicy opportunism of the old buccaneers, and leaves behind their atrocities.

The first buccaneers faced physical risks as part of their profession. The professional risks faced by buccaneer-scholars may not be physical, but they are daunting all the same. No one who flouts authority is likely to receive the rewards, resources, and honors that authority has to offer. As buccaneer-scholars, our exploits may be celebrated, but rarely by the people who give Nobel Prizes or MacArthur "Genius Grants." Conventional thinkers are nervous around buccaneers. Freedom has its price.

Buccaneers and the Enlightenment

The free society of the buccaneers never would have formed or flourished had it not been for the New World. But the discovery of new lands also inspired new intellectual freedom, even in Europe.

It's not a coincidence that the historical buccaneers operated during the period of history in which some of the greatest Enlightenment thinkers—such as Galileo, Descartes, and Francis Bacon—lived. The Royal Society was founded during this age. What was called the "New Philosophy" of modern scientific inquiry began to replace the old-fashioned reverence-for-authority approach known as Scholasticism. Things were loosening up in the world of ideas, and though there were many reasons for that, one of them was the many revelations about new plants, animals, geography, and cultures coming back to Europe from around the world. Assumptions about the nature of the world and the humans who inhabited it were shattered. When the world suddenly becomes larger, all kinds of disruptions may be expected. Buccaneers, and buccaneer-scholars, are disruptive, and they also know how to prosper in times of disruption.

Today, the Internet is a kind of New World, exposing each of us to a wider variety of information and allowing us to make a living and an education in radically new ways. It is the buccaneer-scholars, with their flexible knowledge and skills, who will come to dominate this new world.

In the seventeenth century, the maintenance of social order was vital. Order came from rulers, intent on securing their own power. They did this with their swords, of course. But they also used advertising. Hence, one of the great ideas in the history of propaganda: *The Great Chain of Being.* The chain was a grand hierarchy, with God at the top, kings below, and everything else below that. Everyone in society had a place on the Great Chain. Even dirt had a place. Higher standing on the chain meant you were more perfect, closer to God. The lower creatures were meant to serve the higher creatures, and there was no moving up—where you were born was where you died.

The Great Chain was a successful tool, in its time, for justifying the powerlessness of ordinary people. The buccaneers defied it. Their society was remarkable for its rejection of hierarchy. Most buccaneer cruises were assembled ad hoc from volunteers who also contributed all the supplies and equipment. They elected their captain and could depose him at any time. The captain had authority only in battle. Buccaneers were *practicing* the theory of social contracts years before John Locke or Thomas Hobbes became famous for writing about it.

No one talks about the Great Chain of Being anymore, but modern institutions of learning use its logic to justify themselves. Intellectual buccaneers reject that. Our allegiance is not to institutions, their ranking systems, or their hollow honors. What matters is the quality of ideas.

Among buccaneers, there is camaraderie, collaboration, reputation, and respect. But there is no allegiance.

Intellectual buccaneering is about self-education, but schools are okay, too. Lots of people like school. I've learned in schools, and I've learned from people who were trained in schools. I happily plunder knowledge wherever I find it.

I don't seek the destruction of schools. I am out to dismantle something else: the popular belief that schooling is the only route to a great education, and that the best students are those who passively accept the education their schools offer.

This also extends to the corporate world. In the modern workplace, where ideas matter, we can't rely on education that comes only from the top down. Successful managers don't treat employees like witless drones following simple canned procedures. Instead they create an environment where even the lowest-ranking worker can have a new idea, develop it, and as a result teach the organization something vital. Of course managers should provide teaching, coaching, and direction. But the powerful organization—the powerful society—is that which finds ways to encourage and harness the full creative potential of each individual, regardless of rank. Traditional schooling fails to do that.

I stand for the spirit of abundance and self-determination in learning. My potential education is all around me. I don't beg anyone's permission to seize it.

Who Can Be a Buccaneer?

Anyone. It's not an exclusive club, it's a life choice. The only fundamental requirement is that you take responsibility for your own thinking and learning. You understand that you are not what other people have done to you. You construct yourself.

You can be university-trained and also be a buccaneer-scholar. You can even be a university professor and be one. I know a couple of those. I love the libraries, the projects, the ideas, and the interesting people I find at universities. If it weren't for all the politics, I could be an academic. Fortunately, many university resources are freely available on the Internet.

You can work in a big corporation and be a buccaneer. I worked for several large technology companies and still vigorously pursued my own education, on my own terms, and mostly on company time. I reasoned that it was in the better interest of my employer that I grow ever stronger of mind. My studies brought me into contact with new ideas and skills. My growing library became a resource for others in my department.

I'm a technologist, but buccaneering is certainly not limited to learning about how computers work. Parents can be buccaneers. Lawyers, welders, anyone can be buccaneers. The key idea is that you are self-determined in your education, *whether or not you are institutionally educated.*

Not everyone is comfortable with a buccaneering style of education. Years ago when I managed a team of software testers in Silicon Valley, I instituted a policy of giving each member of the team one day off per week, with pay, as long as they used that day to study something work-related. I was shocked to find that *no one* took me up on that offer. When I asked two testers specifically why they weren't taking advantage of the learning days, they told me, "We would rather go to a class than learn on our own."

They were not buccaneers.

I have to say, the majority of those I teach and work with seem passive in their learning. Most people I talk to are waiting for a teacher or wishing they had the time or money to get this or that credential, when they could be taking their fate into their own hands. They see themselves as waiting and saving their money for passage on an ocean liner that will take them on a safe and conventional guided tour. Meanwhile, all around them, little sailboats like mine are coming into port, and embarking again, on unauthorized and impromptu explorations of the world.

WHY BE A BUCCANEER?

Perhaps, like me, you can't help but be this way, and the question is irrelevant to you. Still, there are advantages to buccaneering:

- A buccaneer's education is not limited by the boundaries of traditional disciplines. We sail right through those boundaries. This gives us access to a richer set of ideas, helps us be successful in multiple fields, and makes us hard to intimidate.
- Buccaneers rethink the labels, forms, and rituals of life. We remix them and make them our own. For us, the wonder of life is continually being refreshed.
- Though it may put us at odds with our conventional-

thinking friends and co-workers, we develop an original point of view that shows us unique solutions to thorny problems.

- We feel at home in our own minds. Our philosophy is self-affirming rather than self-loathing. We don't use slogans like "be disciplined and follow the plan" or "don't procrastinate." Kicking ourselves is not our idea of motivation.
- In our hyper-linked, media-saturated world, the ability to adapt quickly and master strange new ideas has become a survival skill. Buccaneer-scholars excel at rapid research.
- Although some are frightened by mavericks like us, others trust us more, because we are not merely parroting what nameless authorities tell us is true.

Buccaneering is free. There are no prerequisites for being a buccaneer-scholar. No permission or training is required. We can do it anytime, anywhere. There are skills and techniques required to be a *successful* buccaneer, but you can acquire them at your leisure. I'll help you with that.

Are You a Buccaneer-Scholar?

You live free . . .

- **Firsthand knowledge:** When there's a conflict between learning from your experience (exploration, experimentation, observation, or testing) and learning from an authority (lecture, rules, or demonstrations), you choose personal experience.
- **Self-directed learning:** When there's a conflict between following your inner compass (your impulses, obsessions, or intuitions) and following an established plan, even your own plan, you go with the inner compass. Your methods are heuristic, not dogmatic.

You hunt ideas . . .

- **Curiosity drives you:** When there's a choice among ideas or actions of equal merit, you prefer the less conventional and less familiar. You are moved by the power of novel and diverse ideas.
- **Puzzles intrigue you:** You're motivated by puzzles, problems, and mysteries, not routine tasks.
- **Complexity dares you:** You know that if someone else has learned it, you can, too. You suspect that most complex things are really quite simple if you discover the organizing principles.

You win your place in the thinking world . . .

- **You construct yourself:** You don't take indoctrination. You aren't a passive vessel. For you, learning is about ongoing personal transformation, not just fact accumulation. You see yourself as thinker-learner-teacher.
- **You earn your reputation:** You are suspicious of titles and certifications. You establish and maintain your reputation through the merit of your ideas. You want to earn the respect of people whom *you* respect.

4

What I Do and How I Do It

Eleven elements of self-education

One day, while I was writing this book, a lawyer called me with a proposal: "We'd like to hire you to find if a software product infringes our patent. Is that the kind of testing you do?"

I said, "Yeah!" *(I had never tested a product for patent infringement before. But I could test for anything.)*

She asked, "Do you know the technology behind network switching in Windows?"

I said, "Yeah!" *(I didn't know what she was talking about. But I could learn it.)*

Then she asked me to read the patent and examine the product. Look at the first claim in that patent:

"1. A method for dynamically routing data over multiple dissimilar parallel wireless networks that are each monitored for status information, the method comprising: maintaining a priority of each wireless network, the priorities indicating a most preferred path; determining availability of each wireless network based upon status information associated with each wireless network; indicating a current most preferred network from the wireless networks determined to be available, the indication being based upon the network priorities; switching from a current network, which is dissimilar from the current most preferred network, to the current most preferred network during a transmission, at least one of the current network and current most preferred network being time continuous; and remaining connected to the current network for a period of time after switching to the current most preferred network."

Did you read it through? If not, you're in good company: me. According to the Flesch-Kincaid Index, which measures reading difficulty, that text is written at a sixtieth grade level. I found it terribly confusing, at first.

This was a high-pressure learning challenge.

How do you think I felt when I finally forced myself to read all those words? I was being paid three hundred dollars per hour. My client expected me to read the patent and understand it. I didn't understand it. Was I intimidated?

No. By the time you finish this book, you won't feel intimidated by complex and obscure text, either.

31

Complexity and obscurity are illusions. They are figments of mind-shock. For a buccaneer, mind-shock is no cause for alarm. It is a temporary condition, a big wave coming over the bow. There's a splash. I get wet. But steady on the helm, there. She'll pull through.

On first reading, I wasn't sure I was qualified to do the project. The expert on the other side of the case, a professor at a well-respected university, was taken aback to discover his intellectual opponent was a high school dropout.

Guess who won the case.

By the time we went to trial, I had become a wizard of the patent. I wrote a program to separate and index each sentence, clause, and word. I memorized most of the three patents involved, analyzing them over hundreds of hours. I absorbed a dozen books on networking technology. I constructed a dedicated test lab. I studied the underlying instructions that comprised the product, and used a variety of hacking tools to analyze its operation. I was better prepared than the professor. He spent two or three days testing it. I devoted nearly four hundred hours to testing it. I brought in a video crew to film me testing it. I tested it inside out and sideways.

The jury noticed.

The facts were on our side, of course. That helps when you need to win a lawsuit. But here's my point: the reason I plunged into this project, even though I didn't know whether I was smart enough to complete it, was because I knew I was smart enough to *start*. Starting is what matters. I'll be smarter by the finish.

That's one of the benefits of being a buccaneer-scholar. With a nonstop education you are in a position to attack opportunities that sail your way, instead of steering clear with "Sorry, I'm not qualified."

When the lawyer first called me, I was in the midst of writing the key elements of my buccaneering method for this book. That case became a fifteen-month interruption. Now, I'm back to the writing.

Before another lawyer calls, let me tell you what the elements are:

SACKED SCOWS!

(It's an acronym for eleven elements.)

Different buccaneers learn differently. That's fine. This is how *I* do it.

These elements summarize everything I do to educate myself. Each represents dozens of techniques, patterns, tools, and dynamics. With them, I successfully sail through adventures that once would have sunk me.

As you read this, see how these elements mesh with your own way of learning.

The Elements of My Self-Education Method

1. Scouting Obsessively, I discover the sources and tools I will need. *It's more than half of the fun for me. I browse bookstores, skim books, surf the Web, or troll the dictionary. I try things and abandon them. I do all this to have deep resources when I need to learn important stuff fast.*

2. Authentic Problems engage my mind. *An authentic problem is one that I personally care about, not one that someone else thinks I should care about.*

3. Cognitive Savvy means working with the rhythms of my mind. *Thinking operates according to patterns and principles that I use to sail my mind, rather than driving or towing it. Researchers call it "metacognition."*

4. Knowledge Attracts Knowledge, the more I know, the easier I learn. *New knowledge connects with old, inspiring questions that reach toward yet more to know.*

5. Experimentation makes learning vivid and direct. *To experiment is to get close to it, question it, play with it, poke at it, and learn from what happens next.*

6. Disposable Time lets me try new things. *Disposable time is time that I can afford to waste. A great deal of my best work I can trace to doodles, games, watching television, and other so-called wastes of time.*

7. Stories are how I make sense of things. *A story is a meaningful arrangement of ideas. Through composing, editing, sharing, or challenging stories, I advance my grasp of the world.*

8. Contrasting Ideas lead to better ideas. *This means challenging my beliefs with opposing ideas. It means asking probing questions, developing skeptical and critical habits to avoid being fooled or ambushed.*

> **9. Other Minds** exercise my thinking and applaud my exploits. *Even though I'm responsible for my own ideas, I find it fun and useful to listen and respond to other thinkers. I get ideas from other people, then reinvent them for myself.*
>
> **10. Words and Pictures** make a home for my thoughts. *Beneath the level of stories, there are words, pictures, and symbols that embody meaning. I discover and deploy powerful words, take notes, fiddle with diagrams.*
>
> **11. Systems Thinking** helps me tame complexity. *Systems thinking is the art of analyzing complex structures to find simple ones beneath. As a systems thinker, I learn faster because I see connections between what I'm learning and what I already know.*

1. Scouting Obsessively
. . . I discover the sources and tools I will need.

"Scouting" means looking for resources you need to improve your education. In classic buccaneering terms, scouting is wandering the seas in search of prey, following the routes your prey is likely to follow. Scouting is about discovering the *existence* of interesting things. Actually studying them comes later.

Scouting for a buccaneer-scholar never stops. Everything I encounter gets sized up for its value as a learning tool. Scouting fills my waking life. Browsing in bookstores and libraries is scouting, of course. So is wandering through an office supply store or a hobby shop. Web surfing, too, and watching television. Ideas may be seized anywhere.

Scouting is often driven by curiosity. Curiosity is the urge to learn something even though it doesn't seem to be necessary to know it, *at the time.* Curiosity is a survival skill for creatures like us who live by our wits, because we can't predict, in an open and complex world, everything we *will* need to know later on.

I scout for myself. I don't rest with someone else's opinion of the sources and tools I should use in my studies. Although I may listen to other people's lectures, read their summaries, or browse other people's links, I also scan for things that others have overlooked. I scan all horizons from the topmast.

2. AUTHENTIC PROBLEMS
. . . engage my mind.

The old buccaneers said it, "No prey, no pay." They knew what problems they needed to solve, and the skills they needed to solve them.

A problem is any situation where there is a gap between what *is* and what is *wanted.* An authentic problem is *a problem that matters to me.* Other people's problems are not necessarily mine.

The buccaneer Pierre la Grand understood authentic problems. He found a way to motivate his crew before attacking the flagship of a Spanish vice-admiral in the open sea: he sunk his own ship. Now faced with drowning, his eager crew quickly captured the new vessel intact, with all its treasure.

The problems posed by my schoolteachers were rarely authentic to me. They didn't care about solutions to the empty exercises, and neither did I. When I don't care, my mind won't maintain its attention. It swivels like a compass needle back to what is authentic for me.

A problem becomes authentic for me when it threatens my survival or happiness. That's why I only began playing a harmonica when

I was trying to impress my first boss, who was a musician (survival). I continued learning more eagerly when I became good enough to enjoy my own playing (happiness).

A problem can be authentic for one person and not for another. This is the hardest part: figuring out what matters to me. This is the *engagement problem.*

Sometimes I think I've found an authentic problem, and I still can't get interested in it. Then I ask, "So what?"

So what if this problem isn't solved? How will that hurt me? A good test for authenticity is to *ignore* the problem. When I ignore an authentic problem, I'm going to feel pain (for example, running out of money, disappointing someone I respect, or feeling bored). If I can easily ignore it without pain, it can't be authentic.

I learn best when I need to solve a problem *right now.*

3. COGNITIVE SAVVY
. . . means working with the rhythms of my mind.

My mind is a sailing ship, and I wasn't born knowing how to sail it. It won't track directly into the wind. I have to mend the rigging and scrape the hull once in a while. It navigates by the stars and by my inner compass. I must steer it clear of rocks and shoals.

Cognitive savvy means learning how my mind works, so I get more out of it with less effort. Scientists call this *metacognition.* Some of the things I've discovered about human minds:

- They procrastinate. They need time to work. But we can harness that procrastination.

- Minds see everything as a story. Minds work with meanings and significances, not with bare facts.
- Minds forget things. Forgetting makes room for new ideas to emerge. Forgetting promotes re-learning, which helps us learn more deeply and correct our mistakes.
- Minds are naturally irrational. Rationality can be gained through study and practice, but it's unnatural. Instead of logical reasoning (using the rules of logic to draw step-by-step inferences), the natural process of the mind is the more intuitive process of recognizing patterns and constructing analogies.
- Minds want shortcuts. Look out for biases and mistakes in reasoning. We can do this by studying common types of logical fallacies and biases so we can better recognize them. We can also get other minds to review our work.
- Minds go through temporary obsessions. Sometimes we can fall crazy in love with a particular idea or philosophy, then fall out of love a few months later. But we can learn to let that storm sweep over us, knowing that it won't last.
- Minds need structures to hold onto while thinking, learning, acting, and remembering. We can practice building these structures, called *heuristics* when they help us solve a problem, *mnemonics* when they help us remember, *models* or *schemas* when they help us learn.
- Minds need to explore, experiment, and play. School often teaches us that learning should be regimented. They tell us subjects must be divided into disconnected

classes. They tell us that we must study set things for set periods in a set order. My mind doesn't work that way. It leaps from topic to topic like sailors through the rigging of a man-o'-war. How about yours?

- A mind is not one being, it's many. We are polypsychic creatures. That means different parts of the brain are independent agents, loosely coordinated by the consciousness that each of us calls "I." Each mind may be a crew in conflict. Learn to take that inner conflict seriously. Listen to it.

- When we push "the crew" of our minds toward something it doesn't want, we may face mutiny. For me, this can be severe. I become torpid and depressed. This has happened to me a few times, but not since I learned how to sense and respect my inner states.

4. Knowledge Attracts Knowledge
. . . the more I know, the easier I learn.

A common practice among the old buccaneers was "trading up" their ships. A small ship allowed them to capture a larger ship, and that one allowed them to capture a still larger ship. Success attracted more men to crew the larger vessels, too. Success led to power, which led to more success.

I'm a buccaneer of knowledge. Knowledge I plunder, and knowledge I use in my quest to know more.

The things we know aren't a pile of independent facts, scattered like rice grains around our heads. Instead they are arranged in meaningful associations called a *schema*. A schema directs our attention, helps us think, helps us remember. It's like an inner map of knowledge. That's how brains work.

For instance, if a driver gets into a car that he's never driven before, it takes him just a moment to figure out where the controls are and how to drive it. This is because all cars have a similar design. Learn about one car, and the resulting "car schema" will teach you about the next car.

Since a schema helps me learn more about stuff I already know, I deliberately study a wide variety of subjects. The more I know about a *variety* of things, the more easily I will learn a *specific* thing in a pressure situation. My eclectic education is not just useful in itself; it equips me to deepen my knowledge, as authentic problems appear on the horizon. I talk more about this in the Treasure Map chapter.

5. Experimentation
. . . makes learning vivid and direct.

Want to learn about flying an airplane? Try flying a real airplane, or practice in a simulator. Want to learn how electricity works? Get an electronics kit and build some circuits. That's how Michael Faraday did it. Need to learn computers? Get a computer and play with it. About five minutes after the start of my first sailing lesson, I stepped onboard a sailboat. Ten minutes later, I steered into open water.

I'm talking about informal experiments as well as the formal controlled kind that a professional scientist might perform. Experimentation in the broadest sense requires two things: inquiry and observation. To experiment is to interrogate, manipulate, tinker, play, compete, probe, take apart, put together, troubleshoot, and in

40

general get very close to your subject. Plunge in! This is important because my mind doesn't achieve full power unless I take action.

Experiments may be driven by the need to solve an authentic problem, or by general curiosity.

6. Disposable Time
. . . lets me try new things.

The old buccaneers were not keen on discipline and schedules. A lot of them came to buccaneering out of a desire to escape the rigid rules and scant opportunities of naval or merchant service.

Many buccaneer cruises got under way without food in the hold. This was no difficulty, since most crews included a Miskito Indian striker who caught fish and tortoise from the deck. Don't like turtle soup? Raid a hog yard on the mainland. Want to get right to the plunder? Go rob a ship and eat their food. The buccaneers were adaptable, and they had plenty of time. A buccaneer cruise was an improvisational journey.

Adaptability is crucial to buccaneers of knowledge, too. If I make a careful plan at the beginning of my journey, and stick to it, I may miss out on a lot of learning. The beginning is a terrible time to plan. It's the moment of greatest ignorance. In self-directed education, a lot of the value comes from exploiting opportunities that arise well out to sea, once I've seen some things and begun the learning process.

In buccaneer learning, wandering is a necessity, not a luxury. To wander effectively I need *disposable time*. That means time I can afford to waste. I've found that by giving myself permission to pursue things that might not come to anything valuable, more often than not, I eventually discover something really valuable.

I don't want to throw my time away. But without disposable time, I will be too conservative about what I learn. I will suppress my curiosity. With disposable time, I take more risks. Often this brings unexpected treasure.

7. Stories
. . . are how I make sense of things.

Any explanation or description we ever tell or hear is a story. Every fact is either a story or it's embedded in a story. Science is stories. History is especially a story. The buccaneers of history are known to us through the stories told about them, stories they told about themselves, and stories told about the artifacts from their lives. In American culture, the buccaneer story was hijacked by Walt Disney and Peter Pan. Think of buccaneers and immediately Long John Silver and Captain Hook come to mind.

Stories are vital to my education. I read explanations, perhaps an explanation of how a transistor works, the history of Oriental rugs, or how Sargon of Akkad rose to power. What I'm reading is not reality, it's a story. Unlike reality, a story is a construct of someone's mind. Unlike reality, which doesn't care what I think, stories need me. A story I read is nothing until I interpret it. Even "objective" facts require interpretation if I want to do anything with them.

Stories have a flow. Stories are connections among ideas. The author of a story highlights what he believes is relevant and suppresses what he believes is irrelevant by choosing what to say, what not to say, and how those ideas are sequenced and juxtaposed. The structure of a story helps us remember the ideas within it.

To evaluate and learn from news stories, press releases, advertisements, arguments, or anything storylike requires that I practice critical thinking. I must know how to dissect stories.

To persuade others and win credibility, I must become a storyteller.

Earlier I told the story of the historical buccaneers. I highlighted the aspects of that story that I think you need to know, and left many things out that I thought didn't matter. I tried to summarize it so that if you did the research yourself you would look at what I wrote and say "Yeah, that's about right."

But maybe I've misled you. Maybe I've oversimplified it. Buccaneer thinkers learn to be suspicious of other peoples' summaries. Practice by being suspicious of mine. A simple way to do that is to read what I wrote about buccaneers and say to yourself "This is Bach's *story* about the buccaneers. I can accept it for the moment, but that doesn't mean I believe it."

One powerful thing I've discovered about telling stories: they don't just convey information. The *telling* of the story, even just going over it in my mind, also helps me understand it better. In other words, when I "learn a lesson" from an experience, I haven't necessarily learned it—I may only have *received* it. How it sinks in and becomes part of my wisdom is, I mull it over and talk about it.

8. CONTRASTING IDEAS
. . . lead to better ideas.

I love to see things smash together. Galaxies, cars, rocks, atoms, and also ideas. Often, to understand an idea, you need to smash it with a different idea, then see what happens to it. Release the hounds! I have spent most of my career as a software tester, where I get to think of devious ways to smash software with strange data.

Buccaneers did a lot of smashing. Maybe that's why I first began to think of myself as a buccaneering spirit—I prefer a swashbuckling style of thinking and debate.

Pitting contrasting ideas against each other is called "dialectical" learning. Harmony among ideas is important, too; that's what stories are for. But as every good scientist knows, we improve ideas more by challenging them, not coddling them.

I want my own ideas to be smashed, if they aren't good enough. I look for ways to uncover my own mistakes before other people do. I cultivate friends who will help.

Contrasting ideas can be read as a verb phrase, as in "contrasting ideas is fun to do," or a noun phrase as in "contrasting ideas are beautiful to behold." Either way, it helps me to break out of linear, either/or thinking. When I hear an idea, I want to generate alternative ideas and compare them. When presented with a choice between two things, my instinct is to uncover more options, more distinctions, more contrasts. One way of doing that is to discover overlooked dimensions. Should I go right or left? How about going *over the top*? Or *underneath*? *Half* go left and *half* go right? How about *waiting*?

Here are some of the more important tools I use to contrast ideas:

- **Skepticism.** This means embracing inquiry while rejecting certainty. A lot of people confuse skepticism with scoffing. To scoff is to reject and dismiss ideas, but true skeptics maintain openness even to outlandish-sounding notions. Skeptics stand for rich possibilities. This is the original skepticism of the philosopher Pyrrho of Elis. He's one of those ancient Greeks you don't hear much about. Pyrrho's idea was that we can know things in a tentative way, but we can't know anything *for sure*. Our senses are unreliable, personal opinion varies, and even mathematics is subject to error. Pyrrho's advice was to avoid strong commitment to any belief. A healthy skeptic says, "I think I know things, but any particular thing I know may be wrong. Let my inquiry continue."

- **Critical thinking.** This means trying to find the problems with an idea. I trace the evidence supporting a conclusion, and consider how the evidence may have been corrupted, or alternative evidence suppressed. I consider potential biases and fallacies.
- **Lateral thinking.** This is the ability to develop a rich set of alternative ideas, and to bring hidden assumptions to the surface. I read books of lateral-thinking puzzles to keep my skills sharp.
- **Systems thinking.** This means thinking about how things work, especially complex things such as machines, people, or organizations, penetrating their illusions and noticing patterns of behavior. See element 11, below, for more on this.

You already know how to do these things. Learning to do them well is a different matter. That's a lifelong pursuit.

9. Other Minds

. . . exercise my thinking and applaud my exploits.

The historical buccaneers were not solitary creatures. The crew of a ship was a brotherhood, and fleets of buccaneer vessels often worked together to raid towns or capture islands.

I am an independent learner, but like the buccaneers, I'm also social. I am part of a loose-knit crew of fellow rovers. They help find mistakes in my work, and they know how to talk to me so that I won't get angry. They tell me about books they've discovered, send me links to important resources they've scouted, send me their writing to review, and review what I write. We criticize each other, and we listen to each other's criticism because it comes against a background of respect. We make each other smarter.

I learn not only by reading, watching, or doing. I also learn by teaching. The need to explain and demonstrate is a powerful exercise. It works my mind so differently that I am routinely led to discover new depths in familiar subjects.

Once, when I was suffering writer's block on a technical article about measuring the quality of software, my brother Jon announced he would use his "power of ignorance" to help me write it. At the time he worked as a dishwasher and had no experience in the software industry. But just by asking me questions about my article, getting me to teach him the material, he helped me find a new way to explain it, and I quickly finished the piece.

I don't have many trusted colleagues. Maybe twenty. Trust grows slowly. Those few help me the most to maintain my enthusiasm and turn out quality work. Outside my close colleagues, one hundred or two hundred more distant thinkers drift in and out of my sphere, occasionally contributing or asking for help. Then there are paying clients from whom I learn, and total strangers who email me with questions.

What brings someone new into my community? *Reputation.* Reputation is vital. This was true for Sir Henry "Admiral of Buccaneers" Morgan recruiting for a raid on Panama City in 1671, just as it's true for me trying to get a free trip to Sweden to speak at a conference. A healthy reputation is an interesting sort of magnet. It automatically repels people who aren't right for you, automatically attracts people who are.

I develop my reputation by doing good work in a way that other people recognize. I put my articles online. I write a blog. I give interviews. I put videos online. With the power of Google, anyone can find me and my ideas. Before the Internet, scholars had to do intensive personal networking or be part of a large institution in order find each other. Today, finding other minds is a snap.

10. WORDS AND PICTURES
. . . make a home for my thoughts.

Ideas can exist without words or pictures to enshrine them. But words and pictures are powerful tools for learning. They bring thoughts into focus. I practice and refine my words as ardently as any buccaneer ever swung a cutlass. I am never more than one click away from the online *Oxford English Dictionary,* which helps me better understand the stories behind the words I use.

If you were to watch my learning process, the most visible elements of it are words and pictures. When I leave my house, I carry my Moleskine notebooks (the best notebook in the world) and bring my

Sharpie calligraphic pen (a prince among pens). Wherever I happen to be, I pick a problem to work on, and I make lists of words and draw diagrams to describe the problem.

The judicious use of words can intimidate, seduce, or uplift. Learning any new subject or skill often begins with learning its specialized vocabulary. Sometimes a single word can make a huge difference. In my community, the words *exploratory, heuristic,* and *cognitive* often serve as rhetorical cannonballs. By that I mean they shake things up, because they are not yet in common use among software engineers, and they represent a different way of thinking about how to build software.

A good buccaneer is nearly impossible to intimidate with words.

There are several ways to subdue words. One way is to shrug and call it bad writing. Consider this sentence from one of my heroes, Buckminster Fuller:

"We find no record as yet of man having successfully defined the universe, scientifically and comprehensively, to include the non-simultaneous and only partially overlapping, micro-macro, always and everywhere transforming, physical and metaphysical, omni-complementary but non-identical events."

Poor Bucky was a smart man, but a *terrible* writer. I think he meant to say, "Any description of the universe oversimplifies it."

Another thing I might do is normalize my ignorance. That means I say to myself, "Lots of other people don't know what that means, either." There's so much to know, how can I feel bad about not knowing it yet? And why should I think that the author of the text truly understands it, either? This allows me to stay cheerful about my learning even when I feel confused.

Finally, I use instant technology to tame heavy words. Just today

I learned how to read a surface analysis chart from the National Weather Service. This was an authentic problem for me because a major winter storm was approaching. I discovered instructions that mentioned "Prognostic charts of atmospheric thicknesses in the 1000ñ850 hPa range." Sounds technical, but by googling "hPa" and "atmospheric thickness," I deciphered that jargon in minutes. (It refers to the average temperature of an air mass, which is important for charting a weather front.) As I was reading about air pressure, I also encountered the word "isobar" and learned that an isobar is a type of isopleth, which just sounds like a cool word to me. Then for fun I went to the dictionary and found every word that starts with "iso." (This is disposable time in action.)

Since knowledge attracts knowledge, the more you do this, the easier it gets.

11. Systems Thinking
. . . helps me tame complexity.

The final element—the final bit of rigging I need to run my ship of learning—is the skill of understanding how complex systems work. I need to be able to see the underlying simplicity in systems without *oversimplifying* them. This is called general systems thinking (GST).

GST is the science of making generalizations about complex and dynamic systems. Basically, a system is a set of parts that interact: computer systems, buildings, weather, language, people, or sailboats are all examples of systems. Systems are all around us. From single-cell organisms to the universe, general systems thinking is the ability to see what's essential for your purposes, ignore what isn't, and reason about it. It helps me contrast ideas and it helps my current knowledge attract new knowledge better.

To simplify something, I must understand it. I tell myself that simple threads make the fabric of the most complex subject. The pattern will be comprehensible. Even when I'm wrong, by the time I figure that out I've already learned a lot.

If you are in a car race, one way to win is to drive very fast. But if you understand the car as a system, you know that the winning driver is the one who sometimes slows down, stops, and refuels. To find a strategy to win a race requires systems thinking.

Systems thinking is a big subject. Here are some of its parts:

- **Modeling:** A model is an idea that we use as a stand-in for another idea that we wish to manipulate or study. For instance, an architect might make a model of a building to show how it will look when it's built. Or an engineer might make a mathematical model of a bridge to study how it responds to forces acting upon it. Models are central to systems thinking. We model systems in order to reason about them. This allows us to see how things are alike or different; create analogies, diagnose problems, and design solutions; and apply useful labels to objects and behaviors.
- **Dynamics:** Dynamics are how things change and influence each other. In systems thinking, this means looking at why systems are stable or unstable, how feedback loops work, why some systems are so hard to predict or control, and what happens to small things when they get bigger.

- **Observation:** Observation relates to what we can know about systems and how we discover it. To do that we need to know how a system can appear different to different people or from different points of view. We need to understand that what looks simple might be very complicated under the surface, or vice versa.
- **Synergy:** Synergy means that a system is more than the sum of its parts. In systems thinking, we are particularly looking at how the structure of a system, and the interactions among its parts, can lead to surprising behavior.
- **Error and Failure:** Things go wrong, sometimes. Systems thinking also looks at how systems fail, and how we make mistakes when working with them. This includes how we might oversimplify a complex system, and fail to predict how it will behave. It also includes studying how systems decay and how they might be misused or abused.

We all do systems thinking, to some degree. What most people don't know is that it can be systematically learned.

MAKING IT WORK: HEURISTICS AND GREAT SECRETS

The eleven SACKED SCOWS of my self-education method are the skills, activities, concepts, and things that comprise how I learn stuff and, in so doing, construct myself. But how do I put those elements to use? The buccaneer metaphor supplies the final bit:

> **Wind:** *Each day I follow how I feel.* I avoid detailed plans. Instead, I harness my passions, forgive myself when passion fades, relax during the calms.
> **Ship:** *Each day I construct myself.* I review and renew what I am. I work on my skills. I practice explaining myself. I become a little stronger and more resilient.
> **Sea:** *Each day I construct my story of the world.* As I sail the sea that is the world, I add to my knowledge and I correct my errors. The world exists independently of me, but what the world means—what matters and what doesn't—is only in my head.
> **Sailing:** *I apply heuristics instead of following rules.* Like sailing, learning is an activity brimming with choices and possibilities. I can't say, even for myself, exactly what is the best way to go about it. Therefore, my eleven elements are heuristics, not rigid rules. What is a heuristic? It's simply a non-guaranteed way of solving a problem. Like a suggestion. A heuristic may help, or it may not. Heuristics allow me to have something like rules without being dominated by them.

I use heuristics because there are no guaranteed ways to build a mind.

All learning methods are heuristic. But where some people recklessly assume their methods always work, I stay vigilant. I don't "follow" heuristics, I apply them. If anything, heuristics follow me. Not only do I control how I use them, I also create and change them. I watch to see that they are helping, and if not, I do something else.

> **Treasure:** *I seek Great Secrets.* "Great Secret" is the name I give to an idea that transforms what I think, how I work, or who I am. A Great Secret banishes confusion and expands my power. It might be a word, a tool, a phrase, or a model. For example, I once believed that a person could work by following rules or following intuition. Then I discovered heuristics, and realized there was a flexible third way. To me, heuristics were a Great Secret.

Remember the court case? I helped my client win by using SACKED SCOWS. I **scouted obsessively** throughout the case, discovering useful books on networking technology and scouring countless websites. The whole thing was an **authentic problem** to me, because millions of dollars and many jobs depended on me doing the best I could. I applied my **cognitive savvy** by not forcing myself to understand the patents all at once, but rather in gentle stages. I used **knowledge attracts knowledge** in that my previous general experience with computers and networking allowed me to quickly absorb the specialized knowledge I needed for the case. I **experimented** extensively (in my **disposable time**) with different ways of using the disputed product in the case, and that allowed me to discover surprising things about it. The whole process of a court case, I discovered, is constructing truthful **stories** about the evidence, and telling those stories on the stand. Of course I had to think a lot about **contrasting ideas** in order to anticipate what the

53

other side was going to argue. I used **other minds** to help me, in the form of the other experts hired to assist me, and hundreds of hours of conversation with lawyers who taught me about patent law. This was important because in patent cases, **words and pictures** have very specific and pivotal meanings. We spent many meetings debating the words and preparing diagrams to present to the jury. Finally, I used **systems thinking** throughout the process, to reason about the patented technology and how it related to the product under dispute.

SACKED SCOWS helps me every day, not just on big projects. Here's a list of my learning activities during a recent week:

- My son Oliver and I worked through about fifty logic problems. (**Cognitive, Savvy, Disposable Time**)
- A colleague sent me an exploratory testing challenge, in the form of a spreadsheet with a bug in it. I investigated the bug and wrote a play-by-play description of my test process. (**Authentic Problems, Experimentation, Other Minds, Stories, Disposable Time**)
- I wrote a program to create some experimental tests. (**Experimentation, Systems Thinking, Disposable Time**)
- I practiced solving Sudoku puzzles. (**Cognitive Savvy, Disposable Time**)
- I solved a simple problem in conditional probability to refresh my memory of how those problems work. (**Authentic Problems, Knowledge Attracts Knowledge, Disposable Time**)

- I read some of a testing book from 1986 in order to better understand the history of software testing ideas. **(Knowledge Attracts Knowledge, Systems Thinking, Other Minds)**
- I heard about a rocket sent into space from New Mexico, and I wondered how high it would have to travel for me to see it from Virginia. So I derived the formula for calculating the distance to the horizon based on eye level. It's been a long time since I did trigonometry; it was fun rediscovering sines and cosines. **(Authentic Problems, Disposable Time, Knowledge Attracts Knowledge, Experimentation, Words and Pictures)**
- I listened to a few hours of lectures about philosophical trends of the Middle Ages, including exotic-sounding ideas like "Neo-Platonism." **(Knowledge Attracts Knowledge, Scouting Obsessively, Contrasting Ideas, Systems Thinking, Disposable Time)**
- I skimmed six or seven articles I discovered while researching the word "metacognition." I thought they might have something to do with analyzing testing practices and becoming a better tester. **(Knowledge Attracts Knowledge, Contrasting Ideas, Scouting Obsessively, Disposable Time)**
- I received a far-ranging answer to the Wine Glass factoring exercise I had given a colleague (*"Describe all the dimensions of a wine glass that may be relevant to testing it."*), which helped me expand the question into

a better exercise for my students. Then I interrogated another colleague as he worked through the same problem. **(Other Minds, Stories, Contrasting Ideas)**

- I worked on answers to testing questions submitted by readers of my blog. **(Other Minds, Words and Pictures, Stories)**

NO SCHOOLMASTERS. NO FEAR.

When I was young, I was alienated from my own way of learning.

I squandered my energy hating myself because my mind wouldn't work the way my schoolmasters told me it should. Then I discovered that my "bad study habits" could produce great work. *I banished my schoolmasters.*

When I was young, I felt confused and overwhelmed. Complex subjects intimidated me. Fear of failure paralyzed me. Now I live as an intellectual. Ideas are my work. But I didn't conquer complexity, I learned to sail through it. *I banished my fear of learning.*

I discovered most elements of my learning method by accident. Over the years, my mind spontaneously manifested them. I used them unconsciously long before I used them on purpose. I've become aware of the wonderful ways learning happens, and I've experienced success and prosperity living this way. Anyone else could, too. Even though my mind works differently than I was taught that it should, *I've banished my fear that I'm lazy and undisciplined.*

5

Mental Mutiny

I tried to think, but nothing happened

Mr. Bedrin started it. No coaxing or threatening would reverse it. He incited *self-respect*. George Bedrin was my sixth-grade teacher at Fayston Elementary school, in Vermont. I was eleven years old, and my adult self was waking up.

The curriculum was interesting enough. In the midst of the Green Mountains, no ocean in sight, we studied oceanography. For our class project, we picked apples, pressed cider, and sold it by the gallon. We used the proceeds to take a class trip to the Massachusetts coastline and experience a bit of oceanography. Mr. Bedrin invited interesting people to speak with us. I vividly remember a snake expert, with piercing eyes and dramatic voice, telling us about pit vipers.

The school was tiny: sixty-six kids in the whole place. Mr. Bedrin taught grades four through six all in the same classroom. Because the students were so diverse, we used a variety of textbooks. Each of us worked through them at our own pace. There wasn't much lecture. We did projects that involved problem-solving and building. Being

Vermonters, we also spent time in the woods. There was little home-work, few tests, and a lot of variety in the day.

What really set Bedrin apart was how he treated us. His style was to be more *with* us than *over* us. He asked us to do things for him, no orders or threats. The way he taught inspired my loyalty. In sixth grade, I liked school.

As a young man, I was desperate for respect. It was pure sunlight, to me. I basked in it and felt worthy. Most teachers I met before and after Mr. Bedrin, in the public school systems of Michigan, Mas-sachusetts, Vermont, and New York, followed a different theory of student management: ridicule, fraud, dire predictions, manufactured problems, and intense social pressure. Where George Bedrin taught self-respect, most other teachers taught anger.

The very next year, hostilities began. Fayston educated only to sixth grade. Older kids were bussed to a large regional school. Har-wood Union High School was a combined junior high and high school facility that was the polar opposite of Fayston. The place reminded me of the Death Star. ("That's no moon! That's public education!") Even the orientation lecture was sinister. I sat in the auditorium with my fellow newbie seventh graders while a frowning teacher strutted up and down the stage, barking at us. Coming from Bedrin's classroom, the scene was bizarre.

At one point the grumpy man said, "We consider you to be young adults now, and we expect you to behave as such." Think about that: imagine welcoming a guest to your home by saying "I expect you not to steal anything." No one would say that unless the opposite was true. I had a terrible sinking feeling.

School can work, even for people like me, by inviting students instead of forcing them. But invitation is not a popular form of leadership in large public schools and even some bureaucratic and corporate workplaces. From the system's point of view, I was a problem student, an "underachiever." From my point of view, the school system was a prison system.

In its mysterious recesses, my mind began plotting its escape.

STEP 1: DECLARE INDEPENDENCE.

Soon after the start of the school year, I discovered the Thirteenth Amendment.

> Neither slavery nor involuntary servitude, except as a punishment for crime whereof the party shall have been duly convicted, shall exist within the United States, or any place subject to their jurisdiction.
> —*United States Constitution, Thirteenth Amendment*

Aha! When schoolwork is involuntary servitude, it's illegal.

Of course my teachers told me that the amendment does not apply to children. I did not have the wit or skill to make a proper verbal answer at that time.

If only I could whisper in the ear of my younger self, I would tell him to say, "The black letters of the Amendment are unambiguous. If the Supreme Court has decided a case that limits this amendment, then cite it. But if there is such a case, I would still question its moral foundation. The interests of children are under-represented on the Supreme court. Besides, surely you can understand that an enslaved class may rise up from time to time and throw off their chains? Don't you people teach history in this school?"

I didn't know how to talk like that when I was twelve. I remember *thinking* such thoughts, but I couldn't form them into sentences under the pressure of a teacher's glare. What did come out of my mouth was "it does *so* apply" and other mumbles of that sort.

I may not have articulated it, but I did have a powerful nonverbal answer: the *existential imperative.*

Jean-Paul Sartre once wrote, "We are condemned to be free." I heard that somewhere as a kid, and the words came back to me one day during English class. It occurred to me that the school could not control my mind. My cooperation with school was entirely by choice. I was free to cooperate, or to refuse, as long as I accepted the consequences.

GREAT SECRET
My mind is free.

Of course the teachers and administrators responded to this by creating consequences. In more violent societies, this might have been achieved by the threat of physical violence. For dissident kids in Vermont, the authorities were limited to minor social torture and appeals to parents.

Parental appeals went nowhere. My father was absent, and my mother was neutral. It was down to me versus the teachers.

(You're thinking I was a real brat of a kid, right? Well, of course I was! But isn't that like criticizing a toddler for falling down? I was developing character and self-image. It can be a messy and experimental process. If I had to do it over again, knowing what I know now, I think I would be more polite—but also even more extreme in my rejection of school authority.)

STEP 2: REFUSE HOMEWORK.

I hated homework.

I was already busy at home. I read fantasy novels. I made technical drawings of imaginary spaceships, stargazed, tramped around the forest that surrounded my home. I collected rocks and tried my hand at bird taming. I watched a huge amount of television. But whether my use of time seemed worthy to someone else hardly mattered. I believed my time belonged to me. Compulsory homework was theft of my time.

I invoked the existential imperative. I refused to do homework. This triggered the traditional responses: ridicule, yelling, detention periods, parent-teacher conferences.

STEP 3: FAIL TESTS ON PURPOSE.

I like tests. I'm good at taking them.

It was wrenching for me, at first, to intentionally fail them. I had to do it, though, to prove the point: you can force me to sit at a desk, but my mind is free.

Well, you'd think I'd thrown a punch at the teacher. He was outraged. They all were, swarming like angry bees. Another parent-teacher conference was hastily summoned.

I also tried inciting rebellion among my classmates. No success, there. I considered setting fires or vandalizing faculty property, but criminal life seemed to have no future. I considered running away, but I had nowhere to go. I thought about suicide once in a while.

The school continued the pressure tactics.

STEP 4: IMPLODE.

The pressure worked. Near the end of seventh grade, I surrendered. It wore me down to be glared at and ridiculed and ostracized. Ultimately, I agreed to do homework and stop failing tests.

I really tried, too. But nothing happened.

I discovered something monstrous: *my mind was blank*. I opened a book and stared at it. My eyes moved over the words; the words appeared in my mind, and then instantly disappeared, leaving no memory. To my horror, it seemed that my mind had fled.

If you ask me where did my mind go or why did it desert me, the short answer is, "I don't know."

How absurd! How funny! My mind and my ego are two different creatures that share the same brain. All my life I had thought I was one integrated human, but now I knew I was polypsychic. If my analytical intelligence were a ship, it had just capsized, while my ego bobbed helpless on a confused sea.

I lost heart completely. For a few days I was listless. Then I decided, heck, if I can't think anyway, why not pretend I'm *choosing* not to think and at least get some credit for being an indomitable rebel. I continued my rebellion after all, only now I felt like a bystander in the war between my mind and the school system.

This was the low point of my life. Twelve years old, you're supposed to be sprouting. I was imploding. I fell into a terrible depression. During the summer after seventh grade, I was wracked with daily episodes of acute despair. They came over me in a cloud of voices, telling me I'm worthless. My hapless family left me alone. I did little but watch television the entire summer. It drowned out the voices.

At the end of the summer, I was riding into town with Mom, struggling with yet another wave of hopelessness. Looking out the window, I saw a bend in the road. As the bend approached—I can still see it now in my mind's eye—a thought came into my head: *"This is the last time I will feel this way!"* I say it came into my head because it didn't feel like an ordinary thought. It didn't feel as if it came from me. I immediately wondered, how could I know that my depression was over? What a strange thing to say to myself.

But it *was* the last time. The great psychic terrier that had been shaking me in its jaws dropped me. At last!

I had hit rock bottom and felt myself begin to bounce back. But, now what? How does my mind work? How do I coax it to think for me? What does it want? Will it leave me again?

GREAT SECRET

My mind is free, even from me.

63

My mind returned, drifting like a ghost ship into harbor. I could think again, but I was scared to push myself.

This is a defining dynamic of my life. I make my living as an intellectual, but not by using harsh self-discipline. To prosper, I've had to follow my inner rhythms of learning and thinking. I do not force-fit my thought process to someone else's idea of how minds are supposed to work. My mind is not a motorboat that I can point and drive. Maybe other people are like that. Not me. I sail by the wind.

Because there's a gap between my will and my mind, often my mind will wander. This may seem like a limitation. I suppose it is. But it means that I often stumble into discoveries that prove useful and profitable. Today, this is exactly how I make my living. Thinking differently is my competitive advantage.

6

The Silence of the Clams

The value of low-pressure learning

One August morning a few years ago, I took a walk on the tide flat at Eastsound, Washington. The flat ran just on the far side of Main Street, overlooked by cozy hotels and restaurants. The water had receded a good ten vertical feet from the high-water mark, and a lot of sea bottom lay exposed in a gooey, silty mass. According to the tide chart, this was an exceptionally low tide, a perfect time to procrastinate from my writing.

2 August 2004 - 5 August 2004

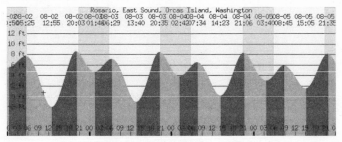

Yes, procrastinate. I was supposed to begin my latest attempt to write what would become the book you are reading now. Original working title: *School Kills.* My dad had suggested that I write it, twenty-two years earlier. Since then, I'd made two strong efforts to get it done. But it hadn't gelled. I was too angry to write about school.

That morning, it had been fourteen years since my last attempt. I finally felt ready, and I was determined to get words on paper. In fact, I had promised to email something to Dad that very night, so he would know I was on the job.

I opened my laptop. Almost immediately my mind sent a strong impulse, "Go for a walk! The tide's out! You love tide pools." My mind sounded irritated. Not the time to be a nag. Sigh.

Notice the S.A.C.K.E.D. S.C.O.W.S.?

- I used procrastination to make progress on my learning while giving my writing an opportunity to simmer in my mind. Later I turned my procrastination activity into material for the very book I was trying to write. (**Cognitive Savvy**)

- I had promised my father I would show him something that night. This is called the Bold Boast technique of gently pressuring myself. (**Authentic Problems**)

- I used Google to discover the tide tables. Modern buccaneers must be as skilled with the Web as the old-time buccaneers were sharp-eyed at the mast. (**Scouting Obsessively**)

A few minutes later I was walking across mats of green leafy stuff (algae? kelp? ick), lots of mud, and about a million broken clamshells. I wondered where all those shells came from. They seemed to be dead, and most of them were in fragments. Did birds carry them here from somewhere else? Were they washed in by the surf? It's a small, sheltered cove, so that seemed unlikely. I thought there ought to be at least some living clams among the multitude of shells. Yet I didn't see any.

As I was musing about all the broken shells, a sudden fountain of water shot up from the muck: a thin jet reaching about four feet in the air. *What is that?* The jet occurred just as I walked by. I wondered at the coincidence. Perhaps I had startled some mud creature? But I'd never heard of anything that squirts water, except possibly squid and the Amazonian Archer fish. There was no sign of a creature where the water came out, just mud and silt.

Then I lifted my gaze to take in a hundred yards of beach, and suddenly noticed fountain after fountain. A dozen at once! The tide flat was in a fit of spitting. Why hadn't I noticed that before? I know I had looked in that direction, earlier, and I had not seen anything remarkable. Yet now I saw them clearly. Another one went off at my feet, and at the same time and place I noticed a dark cylindrical form recede into the muck. Could that be a clam?

Notice the S.A.C.K.E.D. S.C.O.W.S.?

- To learn about the tide flat, I applied a heuristic called "Question Each Detail." That means I picked a pattern in the scene, in this case the shells of dead clams, and I asked myself how that pattern came to be. I

67

imagine alternative possibilities. **(Cognitive Savvy, Contrasting Ideas, Experimenting, Systems Thinking, Knowledge Attracting Knowledge)**

• Once I noticed all the waterspouts, I realized that I had been suffering from what's called **inattentional blindness**. This is the tendency not to see something that is in plain view, because your attention is absorbed by something else. **(Cognitive Savvy)**

I wandered back up to the road and into town. Just a block along, I came upon Darvill's Bookstore and decided to browse. Book scouting is one of my favorite pastimes. I combed through each shelf, looking for books that might confer wisdom, solve a problem, or unravel a nagging mystery.

I noticed a book called *Great Feuds in Science,* riffled through it. Newton versus Leibniz, Hobbes versus Wallis, Galileo versus the Pope. Interesting, but I didn't see an immediate need for the book in my work.

Another book caught my eye, *Evergreen Pacific Shellfish Guide: The Complete Guide for Shellfishing with Crab Fishing Zone Charts and Charts With Beach Listings for Washington & Oregon Waters,* by J. D. Wade. Ah! Clams! I wanted to know about clams.

Zoology doesn't usually draw my attention. Yet, opening the book, I saw that there was apparently quite a bit to say, and the author appeared excited to say it. It often happens to me that being around other people's enthusiasm gets me fired up, too.

I remembered my question: Do clams spit water into the air?

According to the book, the answer is yes. Especially horse clams. Mystery solved. I learned more. Clams live deep in the sand—only dead clams are seen on the surface. Clams have long necks. Wow. I always assumed that clams live completely inside their shells. How could I exist this long on Earth and know so little about clams?

Notice the S.A.C.K.E.D. S.C.O.W.S.?

- Without any particular goal in mind, other than to satisfy my long habit, I browsed the books (**Scouting Obsessively**).

- I remembered a question and skimmed the *Shellfish Guide* to answer it. (**Experimenting**)

- I am often stirred to learn something by seeing someone else's passion for it. The writer engaged me with his exuberance. That's why I kept reading. (**Authentic Problems**)

- Buccaneer-scholars are attracted to puzzles. When I see something that I can't explain, I want to learn about it. This is one of the manifestations of curiosity. (**Authentic Problems**)

A few days after my tide flat adventure, I realized this was an opportunity to study my own learning method. Whatever I discovered would help me write my book. I *thought* I was procrastinating when I played in the mud, but it appeared now that I wasn't.

I had skimmed the clam guide for about ten minutes. Now, shellfish trivia was drifting about my head like the green crab larva (which can move five miles per day and displaces indigenous crab species in the Northwest such as the Dungeness). I hadn't seen the guide since that brief time in Darvill's Bookstore. As a learning experiment, I wondered, what could I recall from it?

Clam Fact	Accuracy
Types of clams include Cockle, Razor, Horse, and Geoducks (pronounced gooeyducks).	TRUE
Razor clams move "fast," at least vertically. "Don't worry, they will not outdig you."	TRUE. Actual quote was *"The clam will not outdig you."*
You can use a shovel or a "clam tube" to get clams. A clam tube is a cylinder with handles on it.	TRUE. Actual description of clam tube was *"A hollow, metal, two-foot long tube, four inches in diameter. It's open on one end, closed on the other, with a half-inch airvent hole and handles."*
There's a paralytic disease you can get from clams (I can't remember the name), because clams concentrate toxins in the surrounding water. It's worse in warm southern waters. Watch out for red tide.	TRUE. It's called *Paralytic Shellfish Poisoning*. But don't forget *Amnesic Shellfish Poisoning*, mentioned in the same paragraph.
Horse clams can squirt water especially far.	TRUE
Horse clams aren't very tasty, except in stews.	*"Actually, they are flavorful when used in chowder."*
Geoducks and horse clams cannot fully retract into their shells.	TRUE
Horse clams can grow to eight inches.	TRUE
Olympic oysters are smaller than other kinds of oysters.	TRUE. But maybe not ALL kinds. *"Olympics are seldom over one and a half inches long, while any larger oysters will probably be the Pacific variety, which can grow to seven inches across."*
Olympic abalone are almost extinct. There's a ban on catching them that will last at least until 2010.	It's actually called northern Abalone in the book (northern not being capitalized, I'm not sure if it's their official name). The book doesn't mention extinction, just a decline in numbers. I got the date right, anyway.
Oysters like to attach themselves to dead oyster shells. That's why it's good to shuck oysters on the beach and drop the shells.	TRUE

I made a list of every shellfish fact I could think of in a few minutes of trying (see table). Then I ran back to the bookstore, bought the book, and scored myself. On the left is what I remember; on the right is the status of that memory compared to the book.

As you can see, I have an imperfect memory. I mixed up or forgot potentially important details (confusing oysters with clams). Considering that the book is ninety pages long, I didn't absorb even 1 percent of it. And yet I felt pleased. One reason is that I learned more

Clam Fact	Accuracy
To find clams, look for their "show" which are holes in the sand. The bigger the hole, the closer they are to the surface.	PARTLY TRUE. The bigger the hole, the bigger the *clam*. When the clams are close to the surface, the show will have a halo.
Some clams, like the horse, can be as much as 18 inches below the surface of the sand.	TRUE
Some clams are found only in 60 feet of water.	That's true of *scallops*; the book doesn't mention clams.
There are a limited number of legal clam digging spots in the northwest. Eastsound, WA is not one of them.	Actually, Eastsound *is* on the map. It was so small I had missed it on my first look.
Clams may be more toxic after severe rains cause more sewage runoff than normal.	TRUE
Clams change their gender every four years.	That's true of *oysters*. The book doesn't comment on clam gender.
It is illegal to possess only the head of a geoduck—you must have the shell and body, too.	TRUE
Clams live in the intertidal zone.	TRUE, and also outside it.
Something about softshell clams...	TRUE, there is such a thing as an Eastern Softshell clam.
Green crabs have five spikes on the front of their shells.	*"five spines..."* (they looked like spikes to me) *"...on either side of the leading edge of their shell."* That means ten total.
If you find a green crab, don't return it to the water.	TRUE
Green crabs are bad.	TRUE, if bad means that they wipe out the scallop industry and other crab species.
Some green-colored crabs are not actually green crabs.	TRUE
Female crabs have a wider abdominal flap.	TRUE
One of the stages in the life of a clam is called a "set."	That's true of *oysters*. No information is given about the lifecycle of clams.

than I expected. When I started making the table, I predicted I'd recall fewer than six facts from the whole thing. Remember, I just skimmed the book for a few minutes. But as I wrote, ideas popped spontaneously into my head, as if the Muse of Clams herself was whispering to me.

In a scouting situation, what matters is the *schema*, not the facts. The purpose of skimming a book is to construct a simple schema (a mental map), or connect to one I already have. In other words, I build a kind of simple clam story in my mind so that specific facts can stick to it. I remembered more facts than I expected to, so the schema must have taken root. Otherwise I would have remembered almost nothing.

Skimming the book extended the meager sea-life schema already in my head, and now included information about how to discover which beaches in Puget Sound are good for clam digging or how to cook clams. I learned about a new category of habitat, and there was a new entry in my mental list of hobbies people might pursue.

How Did Clam Lore Improve My Life?

There are four levels of goodness here:

1. The value of learning about clams.
2. The value of learning about anything.
3. The value of reflecting on my way of learning.
4. The value of telling you about it.

All four put together mean that my little procrastination walk paid off nicely.

1. The value of learning about clams

I don't yet know the value of learning *specifically* about clams. Perhaps one day clam trivia will help me survive on a desert island.

2. The value of learning about anything

Learning about anything, even clams, slightly extends and improves my *future* learning about *other* subjects. New knowledge sticks better when it connects with what I already know. As the byssal fibers of the *mytilus edulis* anchor it against crashing waves, so clam knowledge may help bind the rest of what I know into a more cohesive and accessible whole.

This is true not because of anything particular about clams. It's true whenever I learn something new and different from what I already know. I'm talking about clams now, but I do this sort of learning every day. It all adds up—actually, it multiplies and interconnects.

I'm a *syncretist*; a systems thinker. I look for connections between things. I love analogies. One thing leads me to another. When I began writing this paragraph, I looked up the definition of syncretism. Then I remembered Joseph Campbell, the famous syncretist, and that reminded me of one of his favorite books, James Joyce's *Ulysses*. It's supposed to be one of the most labyrinthine books ever written. It's available online, so I read the first chapter, where Buck Mulligan mentions the importance of reading Homer in the original Greek. I once studied Greek, and that reminded me of a whole other learning story that I could include in this book . . . Now I'm back to finish the paragraph. Whew!

(My editor suggested that I delete the preceding paragraph because it seems like a tangent. No, no, no. It looks like a tangent, but it's really a demonstration of how thoughts connect to thoughts. It's mental windsurfing!)

For me, the world is connections, reflections, fractals, and self-similarity. I think this way partly because I can't help it. My mind has a shallow keel, a short rudder, too many sails. But it also gives me a certain advantage in the marketplace of ideas. Conventional thinkers have to compete on price, since their strategy is to have the same product as everyone else. I compete on uniqueness.

I was trying to think of how I could best illustrate this point, when a challenge came to mind: pick any subject at random and find a fact that relates that subject to clams.

The first problem I have is how to pick a subject at random? I remembered (from scouting I did years ago) that the *Encyclopedia Britannica* includes an "Outline of Knowledge." It is a concise list of subjects encompassing nearly all general knowledge. A few Google searches later, I found a copy of it online.

I wrote a little computer program to choose a topic at random from the outline. When I ran the program, it spit out "artificial fibers." So how are clams related to artificial fibers? Clams are mollusks. It took a few minutes of searching to discover something called *byssal fibers* which are found in certain mollusks and used to make a very fine fiber called *sea silk*. Apparently there are just a few people on the island of Sardinia still harvesting and working with this stuff.

Researching that led me to a 1997 science article:

> Researchers have isolated the protein producing the uniquely strong collagen that allows mussels to stick so aggressively to everything from rocks to oil-rigs . . . An improved understanding of byssal threads might help scientists design biomaterials that take advantage of their remarkable properties, says Harold Slavkin, director of the National Institute of Dental Research, one of the National Institutes of Health, which sponsored the study. "Insight into the molecular structure that makes the byssus strong yet flexible might suggest, for example, new strategies for designing more comfortable and pliable artificial skin."

Isn't that cool? My search for connections was rewarded. This reward increased my confidence, matey. The feeling of learning, whatever the subject matter, is itself a rush of power. It's a demonstration of strength, an affirmation of spirit. It's proof of new choices in my future. The clam episode was not just about clams, to me. It was about catching learning in the moment it happens and exalting in it.

3. The value of reflecting on my own way of learning

What's better than a feeling of power? The feeling of *meta*power! The power to get more power. When I analyzed my clam learning and wrote down my story, more of my own approach to learning became clear to me. I strongly recommend doing this. When I wrote the first part of this chapter three years ago, it was the very first text of this book. That writing led me to reflect deeply on my learning method. It took me three years to tease out all the elements. That helped me develop a self-education seminar (is that a contradiction?) and inspired me to apply this sort of learning analysis to my work as a software tester. And it all began with the clam thing.

4. The value of telling you about it

This book itself is an asset to me, but more valuable is that some of you, reading this, will be inspired to take these ideas even further.

THE PRINCIPLE OF PERIPHERAL WISDOM

Can there be any doubt about the value of my clam walk? I learned a *tiny bit* about an *apparently useless* subject for *apparently no reason,* yet good things came of it. I'm still reaping benefits.

Notice that the benefits are all side effects of my actual purpose, that day. Remember what my purpose was? I took a walk on the tide flat because I was trying to avoid writing this book.

GREAT SECRET

*Most of my learning
is a side effect.*

The Principle of Peripheral Wisdom says that most of what we learn is a side effect of something else we were trying to do.

This principle works because the experience of living doesn't just teach lessons, it teaches many lessons simultaneously. Reality demonstrates itself in manifold ways every moment, like radio waves passing through a receiver whether or not that receiver is tuned in. What learning we gather is limited only by our imagination and motivation.

The more skilled I am at analyzing my experiences and recognizing lessons, the more I can gain from anything that occurs. Sometimes I even seek experiences specifically because they are likely to be rich with useful, unplanned peripheral lessons.

By expecting to learn the unexpected, I can multiply the value of whatever happens. Then I feel more in control of my life, because I feel I can make anything into a productive learning experience—no matter how unwelcome or unpleasant it seemed to be at first.

How to use peripheral wisdom:

- To appreciate all you know, don't stop with things you studied on purpose. Also recognize what you learned that you didn't *try* to learn.
- When assessing a particular educational experience, look at the surprising lessons that came out of it, not just the expected ones.
- If you go through a terribly embarrassing experience, take comfort in the thought that a few days or years from now, you'll be able to use it as a funny teaching story. Your students will say, "Even *you* screwed up? Maybe there's hope for *us,* after all!"
- When your planned learning is frustrated or interrupted, ask "what different sort of learning can I *easily* do in this situation, even if it wasn't my original choice?" (See The *Follow the Energy* Heuristic and The *Long Leash* Heuristic, later in this chapter, for details.)

So if I set out to learn the art of etymology, but instead learn about the architecture of knitting procedures (that happened to me last month), my strategy is to shrug and enjoy my new appreciation for the technical skills of serious knitters. I draw a bull's-eye wherever my arrow happens to land.

PERIPHERAL WISDOM WHEN THINGS GET ROUGH

I'm serious when I say that I learn from any experience, no matter what. I don't seek unhappy experiences, but I insist on gaining maximum benefit from them when they happen. I want all my friends and kin to be safe and healthy, but when my sister was killed in a car accident, I learned how to live through grief. I lock up my belongings, but when my apartment was ransacked, I learned about criminal psychology and the justice system.

When my wife, Lenore, had emergency surgery and the doctors thought she had cancer, I learned about the strength of our marriage. I learned how large hospitals work. I learned greater trust for my friends and family. Once we discovered the problem, I put myself through a crash course on endometriosis. I found out why a doctor who gives you wonderful news may not smile (it's because he is about to give very bad news to the family sitting next to you in the waiting room). I spent every night in her hospital room, sleeping on a chair, and each day roamed the bookstores of Seattle.

To learn from whatever happens, no matter how horrible that experience may be, is a kind of revenge on bad fortune that is always available to us. I learned this attitude at a very young age from my father. I know it will serve my own son well, as it has served me.

Today Lenore, using her peripheral wisdom, tells me it was a good thing that she had to be rushed to the hospital and almost died. It forced me to fly home and cancel all my work, which is how I got the free time to finish writing this book.

THE PRINCIPLE OF ALTERNATION

Consider breathing. Inhaling makes exhaling work. Exhaling makes inhaling work. They are interdependent. Our breathing is a cycle, but not a futile cycle, because it drives oxygen into our bloodstream.

It's a cycle that drives us forward. Breathing illustrates what I call the Principle of Alternation.

The Principle of Alternation states that any one activity may *lose* its value the more you do it, while *increasing* the value of a complementary activity. By alternating what we do, we can make better progress. Alternation is part of the Contrasting Ideas element of my buccaneering method.

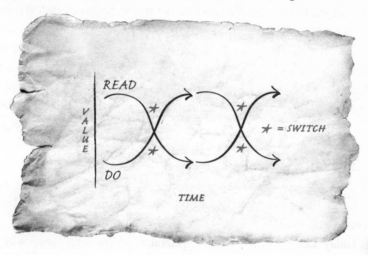

This is a big part of how I learn. I mix complementary learning activities, sometimes switching between them rapidly. For instance, to learn technology, I alternate rapidly between reading about it and playing with it.

Notice in the clam experience I bounced through several things. I tried to write, then took a walk and experienced the clams, then browsed a shellfish book, then let it drop, then went back to the writing, then went back to the shellfish book, and back again to the writing.

I let what I wrote about that incident sit for *two years* before editing it once again.

Because I understand and accept alternation, I no longer waste my energy trying to push to a conclusion on a learning activity that my mind has grown tired of. I no longer see that as a problem, or a failure. It's just a signal from my mind that it's time to switch things up. It's a signal not just that it is tired of something old, but that my mind is *primed* for something new.

The alternation dynamic can manifest in different ways, including:

- "Do A, then B, then A, then B . . ."
- "Do A, then B, then C, then D, then A . . ."
- "Do A, then anything *not* A, then A"
- "Do A, then repeat A, then repeat A again . . ."

Alternation is forgiving. I like that. If you miss the tide, don't worry, there will be another one. Come to think of it, forgiveness is also part of a cycle, and also important to learning. When I forgive myself, I accept the past without being bound to it. I turn bad memories into resources.

Many of my learning heuristics make use of alternation. Look for it.

The *Follow the Energy* Heuristic

For most of my life, I have used alternation—and felt terrible about it. I thought it was a sign of a broken mind. The better way to learn,

I believed, would be to concentrate and read every word in one entire book before moving on to a different book. Finish what I start, you know? I thought having ten books on my desk at one time meant my attention span was weak.

I didn't understand that I was stuck in the "conduit metaphor" of learning. It's an old idea: teacher has knowledge; teacher packages knowledge into "delivery trucks" of words and sentences; trucks bring packages to brain; brain unloads trucks, stores knowledge on mental shelves, waits for more trucks.

In terms of the conduit metaphor, knowledge is the same for everyone; it is transferred by memorization and conditioning. From that point of view, my learning style is insane: Trucks crowded together, abandoned, half-unloaded. Knowledge strewn about as if the trucks and cargo had been hit by a flash flood that struck and receded without reason or warning.

In 1995, that changed. I began to study exploratory thinking, heuristic reasoning, the dynamics of play. I was looking for a more systematic way to explore and learn complex technology. What my research revealed stunned me: *play already is systematic.* Exploration follows its own order.

The conduit metaphor may work for plain memorization (say, studying for a spelling bee), but it's hopeless for the kind of education I want. Fortunately there's a better metaphor available: construction. Maybe knowledge isn't delivered, but rather constructed actively through my experiences. Then my apparently flighty learning style would make sense. What looks like pickiness and fickle attention is my mind searching out the special materials it needs, then piecing them together into a way of seeing the world, and building more complex and interesting structures.

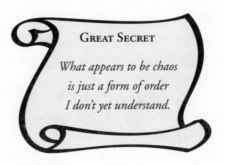

Great Secret

*What appears to be chaos
is just a form of order
I don't yet understand.*

Buccaneering is a "constructivist" philosophy of learning. By studying learning from that perspective, I began to see the critical role of *hunting*, rather than passive acceptance. I began to see a crafty intelligence behind the urge of curiosity. Curiosity is one way my mind hunts. Then it dawned on me that my "weak attention span" is not so weak. It's the opposite. My attention span is so *powerful* that it dominates my ego. My mind is a rhino in a restaurant, pushing over tables, nuzzling the food, grazing on the salad bar. My conscious will is the scandalized maître d' pleading and flapping at it with a napkin.

Now I see a method to my wandering. The method requires alternation and diversification. It requires production and pursuit of many ideas. It requires the wisdom to abandon many of them, too. It requires that I appreciate my peripheral wisdom. The role of my conscious mind is to gently facilitate this process.

How can I manage alternation so that it doesn't fly out of control? I follow my energy. Energy is the telltale.

How do I know what I should be doing right now? I consult my feelings. When I propose various courses of action, my feelings respond with indifference or with excitement. The feelings may be subtle. I may have to sit quietly to detect the message. Sometimes the feelings are not subtle at all, which leads to a phenomenon I call "springboard procrastination." That's discussed in Chapter 7. Follow the Energy is how I know when to switch tasks when I'm alternating. I don't fight through sleepiness. I don't yell at myself when I'm bored. I just let my mind do something else. We'll come back to that later.

To ignore my energy would be as absurd as a sailor ignoring the wind.

By following the energy, I'm watching the rhino, figuring out that it wants more sprouts from the salad bar, and rushing to bring them before the animal shoulders through the kitchen wall to get them.

When I practice buccaneering as part of paying work, my conscious will plays a vital role. It negotiates the conditions that will give my mind the room and resources it needs. As a result, my work is inventive; the intellectual property I create is unique and valuable, and my clients and colleagues are pleased.

THE *LONG LEASH* HEURISTIC

What if you have a really strong will and the ability to focus on whatever seems worth learning? Sometimes that describes me, too. No more rhinoceros: now it's a little dog. Think Sheltie, or Jack Russell terrier.

When I can command my mind, I'm careful not to command it too heavily. I treat it as if my little dog and I are walking in the woods. I stick to the trail, but the dog heads sideways to investigate the bushes. I could say "Heel!" or keep the dog on a short leash, but I use the Long Leash heuristic, instead.

Long Leash means that I encourage my mind to wander, but every ten minutes or hour (depending on how much Disposable Time I have) I tug on the "leash" and get back to work. We work for a while and then my mind wanders again. This repeats.

The essence of Long Leash is to say yes to distractions. I cultivate responsible distractibility.

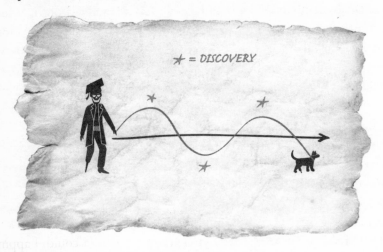

What does this heuristic do for me? It allows me to get my work done while creating opportunities for happy accidents to improve my work. Long leash is a peripheral wisdom heuristic.

When I first discovered the Long Leash method of productive wandering, I set an alarm clock to ring every fifteen minutes. When the clock chimed, I would bring my mind back to my purpose. After a couple days of that, I discovered that the fifteen-minute timer had entered my head. I would spontaneously remember to refocus. I no longer needed a clock.

Sometimes I am surprised to discover that my little dog has morphed back into the rhino. It charges into the forest and I am dragged along. At that point I invoke Follow the Energy. In other words, control can shift back and forth between my executive self (what I also call my ego, conscious will, the great and powerful "I," or the buccaneer) and my analyzing self (which I also call my mind, my thinking self, or my ship).

Learn to guide it without fighting it.

GREAT SECRET

*I can learn on purpose while also
creating opportunities to
learn by accident. I do both!*

7

Happy Learning, James!

Discovering my passion; overcoming my fear

When I was fourteen, my father sent me a computer: an Apple II+ with 48K bytes of memory—that's 393,216 ones or zeroes. A city of bits. It seemed like a lot. Plus, the processor ran at one *mega*hertz. A million actions each second.

Just as someone who wins the lottery might envision bathing in money, I wanted to clothe myself in the delicious bits and hertz of my computer.

But before Dad sent the computer, he sent the manuals. I still remember the smell of them, and the beautiful Apple logo. I felt like Dorothy coming out into colorful Oz. I devoured them. It was the opposite of the trouble I had with homework, when each sentence instantly disappeared from my memory: this material burst through my mind like fireworks. I read the text, understood it, saw it explode with implications and uses.

Days later my brother Jon noticed strange boxes in our garage, each clearly stamped with the Apple Computer logo. Somebody delivered them without telling me! We charged into the house with them ("be careful be careful be CAREFUL") and tore everything open.

What wonders! Futuristic, tan-colored plastic. Implacably intelligent black-and-white monitor. A keyboard full of keys—each one must do something. Imagine that: each key is a unique message to the computer brain by which I shall communicate my thoughts and wishes. A graphics tablet with an electric pen and graduated surface. A box called a "disk drive" connected to the computer. What does it do? How do you work it? Do these flat square things go inside it? Consult the manual. No time for that! Match the cable to the slots that they fit. Put the square thing (a disk?) into the disk drive—no, that must be backward because it won't go in—yes, that's the way—turn the power on. Is it supposed to make that loud rattle?

Is it on now?

Try stuff! Press each key. Twist the game paddles. Type RUN. Type CATALOG. Type LIST.

About young men: boys like me want to be masters of our own universe. That's why we love comic books, role-playing games, and action movies. A computer is a universe; self-contained and complete. It makes sense that most hackers are men; it satisfies something deep. The ancients sent their boys to wrestle cave bears. Today we wrestle Microsoft products.

For me this need was magnified because I felt so little control over my life. I was in a cold war with almost every adult in my life (except my father, who didn't live near me) and with many other kids my age. The new computer had a mesmerizing, almost narcotic effect on me. Like cocaine, it kept me up all night. Like LSD, it gave me visions. Like morphine, it swept away pain.

"LIST" That's how I fell in love with computers. About four months before Dad sent me my first computer, I was at the Vermont Amateur Telescope Makers convention with a friend of my stepdad, Mr. Schwittek, who worked at IBM. As we wandered about in the midst of hundreds of wooden tubes and glass lenses—each one depressingly not owned by me; and every one untouchable, inaccessible, and generally contributing to my boredom—we came upon a lone computer sitting on a table by itself, a tiny white block blinking in the corner of its screen. To my delight, Mr. Schwittek knew how to work it. He walked up to it and touched the keyboard like Spock on *Star Trek*. The computer instantly came to life. Hundreds, thousands of inscrutable words and symbols leapt up from the bottom of the screen like sparks from a bonfire, scrolling off the top again.

"What did you DO?" I asked in wonder.

"Oh, I typed 'list,'" he said. "It's a command that displays the program that is currently in memory."

Commands! Displays! Programs! In that moment, I became the boy who would be king of computers.

A LEARNING FRENZY

I was obsessed.

I wish I still had the software I wrote in the early days of this enchantment. I tried something new with each program I created.

My first program was designed to draw the shape of a planet's orbit around the sun. I sketched it out on paper during the excruciating time between receiving the manuals and finding the computer. I sweated and doted over it. Writing it, rewriting it on clean paper, simulating it in my head, discovering and fixing problems. The computer language I used (imagine that, computers speak a mysterious language of their own) called Applesoft BASIC, was built into the Apple II. When finally I typed the program, instruction by instruction, into the glowing vitals of the system, it was a perfect work. It remains one of the very few programs I've ever written in my career that worked exactly as it was supposed to on the first try.

Apart from playing with planets, I also bought a computer game called "Adventure." The game simulated a little world described in text. The game told me where I was and what was happening; then I could type commands like "go north" or "get sword." When I started that game for the first time, my mind whirled with the possibilities. The game placed me in a room in a little house. It described the room. I began typing commands . . .

One week later I was in the same damn room. I couldn't get out! I tried every command I could think of: GO OUT; GO SOUTH; LEAVE ROOM; OPEN DOOR; BREAK DOOR; DESTROY WALLS. Finally, in disgust, I hacked into the game program itself and rewrote it so there was a hole in the North wall of that starting room. Then I restarted the game, typed GO NORTH, and so escaped. I felt clever, but less clever later on when I discovered the correct method for leaving the room was to type EXIT.

Such absurd narrowness! How stupid the program was. I was discovering many limitations in my computer by then. My dreams were too ambitious, and my computer seemed slower and smaller every day.

I wanted more control over the computer, more speed, and there was a way to get it. Beneath the Applesoft language, there is another language, much faster and with greater control over the computer: *Assembly Language.* Assembly Language is what the microprocessor itself speaks. It's the language of the computer's innermost thoughts.

Despite my lust to take further control over my computer world, I was intimidated by Assembly Language. It frightened me because the same IBM engineer/astronomer who introduced me to computing also told me, "Assembly Language is very difficult. Only the smartest programmers use it." So in my mind, if I tried and failed to learn Assembly, it would prove I was too stupid to be a real computer guy.

My father was not frightened. Although he had never programmed a computer in his life, he seemed to think that learning to speak the native tongue of computers would be easy. He found a book called *6502 Assembly Language Programming* and sent it to me. That's Dad. He's as light as a butterfly sometimes. Practical difficulties don't concern him. If you want to do something, then just start doing it.

The Experiment That Changed My Life

The book was emotionally radioactive. I couldn't throw it away, because it was a gift. I couldn't bring myself to read it, because it might prove me a dimwit. For six months it lay undisturbed, sinking into the clutter of my room.

On a spring day in my fourteenth year, as I was gathering up dirty laundry, I noticed the book again, peeking out from under my bed. I felt a stab of guilt that I had not yet read it. A familiar feeling. Then something new happened. An image drifted into my mind. I saw the sentences in the *6502* book as a path of stepping-stones across a turbulent river. Each idea in the book was a stone on that path, one sentence leading to the next. To learn the computer's language, I must hop from stone to stone. If the material was too hard, there must be a moment in the book (a sentence? a word? a punctuation mark?) where the gap was too wide to leap.

Maybe if I hopped very carefully, I could find a way across. I proposed to myself an experiment: I would read the first chapter slowly, one sentence at a time, studying each diagram. I would travel the stones until I found where my comprehension could go no further. I would study that gap in the stone bridge, and maybe find a way past it. I believed I couldn't learn 6502 programming, but maybe I could discover *why* I couldn't learn it.

It was difficult to open the cover of the book. I stared at it a long time. When I finally did open it, I was startled to discover Dad had written a message. "Happy learning, James!" As if he'd been waiting for me to start this experiment.

I opened to the first page of content and started reading. Easy stuff, as I expected. But then more easy stuff came after that. The author was explaining what a computer is. This was nursery school level. In less than two minutes I dropped my sentence-by-sentence crawl and skimmed ahead, scouting for hard stuff. It had to be there, right?

Then my eyes found a paragraph that changed everything:

"Instructions often frighten microcomputer users who are new to programming. Taken in isolation, though, the operations involved in the execution of a single instruction are usually easy to follow. The purpose of this chapter is to isolate and explain those operations."

—*Lance Leventhal, 6502 Assembly Language Programming*

It was like coming in out of a blizzard. Like hot cocoa for my soul. I read this and thought, *Of course I can learn Assembly Language programming.* The author had anticipated my worries. He's saying it's normal to feel apprehensive, and this apprehension will pass.

Suddenly, I wasn't afraid of a little confusion. Bring on the hard stuff, Leventhal. But I would discover no hard stuff in the whole book. Everything was methodically explained. Each point led easily to the next, with diagrams to reinforce the text. I wrote a little Assembly Language program. It worked. I wrote a bigger one.

I did it. I crossed that river. Less than two years later, I was developing computer games professionally. I got the job because I knew Assembly Language.

Dad had been right. It *was* happy learning. I felt smart. When I feel smart, I invest more energy in learning, and then I do better. Therefore, I *am* smarter when I feel smarter.

GREAT SECRET

*At a distance,
many fun things to learn
look scary.*

That was one of my earliest experiences with cognitive savvy. Instead of using brute willpower to "buckle down and study," I used a gentle touch:

- I let my mind run away from the book until it signalled it was ready to engage. The signal came as a feeling of mild curiosity about the book, a relaxing of the fear.
- I protected my self-image by casting the learning process as an experiment. No matter how badly the experiment came out, I could tell myself it was "just an experiment." That gave me some emotional distance.
- Having created an *emotional* distance, I was able to eliminate the *cognitive* distance: I brought myself as close to the material as I could get. I read every word and convinced myself that I understood each one before I moved on. I had "plunged in," and to my surprise, immersing myself in the book was far more pleasant than I feared. What looked hard from afar turned easy when I stopped running.

- I gave myself an escape route. When I have a way out, I feel more courage to rush in.
- I put the knowledge to use by writing programs and seeing that they worked. This filled me with new energy to keep studying.

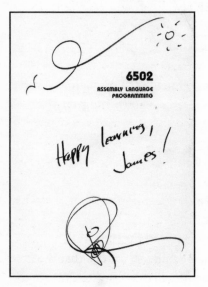

CYCLIC LEARNING

The stepping stone image helped me, but I only needed help because I didn't understand *cyclic learning.* I believed that knowledge should be gained in an approved sequence. I believed that breaking the sequence would prevent me from learning, or at least condemn me to a shallow, unsatisfying skill.

The stepping stone idea is too simplistic. Rarely must knowledge be gained in a strict sequence of facts. Cyclic learning means learning in broad stages, progressively filling in the gaps and resolving loose ends. But the stages don't need to be pre-determined or rigorously sequenced.

Here's how it works:

1. **First pass.** Encounter the material and try to understand it. Some of it I might get. Some of it I won't. *Don't worry!* Smile. Relax. If I feel confused, I just keep going as if nothing is wrong.

2. **Review what I know.** Honor my progress. Just because I don't know everything doesn't mean I'm completely ignorant. Confusion is not a black mark, *it's a bookmark*—it tells me where I still have work to do.

3. **Pause and do something else.** The pause may last a few moments or a few years.

4. **Next pass.** Go through the material again. See if any of the confusion has been spontaneously resolved. If not, I pick one of the gaps and work the problem. I may use Google for this, or talk to someone, find a different book, ask questions, try an experiment.

5. **Pause again.**

Cyclic learning is a constructive process, progressively sculpting my mind. My knowledge begins crude-hewn, but with each pass new information and finer distinctions refine it. Notice how cyclic learning embodies the Principle of Alternation. Notice that the Follow the Energy or Long Leash heuristics may be used to manage the process.

The key to success in cyclic learning is to suspend self-judgment and tolerate confusion. I couldn't do that when I was very young, because I secretly feared that I was stupid, and I thought confusion would prove it. Today I have three big advantages over my young self: I know I *can* be smart. I know I *can* be stupid. Either way, I know I *am* worthy.

Cyclic learning looks chaotic to the novice self-educator, just as the workings of a sailboat seem chaotic the first time you experience them. With practice and experience, you learn to read the trim of the sails.

GREAT SECRET

If I try to understand, but fail, that's progress.

Cyclic learning means that I can study stuff, *fail to understand it*—and still call it successful learning! But how can "failing to understand" be successful learning? Several ways:

- **There is progress in failure.** There's a huge difference between not knowing about something that I've *never* looked at, and not knowing about something I *have* looked at. Just looking at it is progress, because my ignorance now has a focus. Instead of "I don't know anything about meteorology," my self-assessment becomes, "I don't yet know the difference between a hectopascal and a millibar" along with fifty other specific ignorances. Failing to learn may be *successful* scouting.
- **Learning in my sleep.** My unconscious mind is like a digestive enzyme that sets to work on objects of confusion. Eating away, eating away. My mind is slow sometimes, but so relentless. Mysteries cannot be left alone. Puzzles must be solved.

- **Inspiring people to help.** If I ask for help from experts, they will be more likely to assist if they see that I've already tried to learn for myself.
- **Helping people learn.** If other people are working with me as I learn, perhaps seeing me fail to understand will help them understand the subject better, or in a new way. A teacher seeing me struggle may be inspired to produce a fresh example or a new teaching activity.
- **Delayed action learning.** What confuses me now may become powerful knowledge in retrospect, even years later, when some new fact or problem arises. We're used to this from mystery stories, right? We encounter clues. We don't know what the clues mean, at first. But we may learn about a new bit of evidence that explains all those clues. A detective must hold confusion patiently in mind, to solve the crime.
- **Rethinking my expectations:** Perhaps I am expecting too much from myself. Perhaps I'm expecting the wrong things. Maybe my failure is just an artifact of focusing on the wrong things. Failure challenges me to rethink what success might be.
- **My puzzle, fragment, or failure could be someone else's solution.** This is powerful, because it means that cyclic learning can span the minds of many thinkers.

An example of this is a brainteaser I once encountered. My brother and I both tried to solve it. Here it is:

Question: ABCDEFGHJMOPQRSTUVWXYZ

Answer: _____

Try to solve this before reading on . . .

My brother Jon worked on this for five minutes or so, then gave up. Ha ha. I'm going to win. I worked on it for ten minutes, and discovered a plausible answer: "the set of all letters that don't spell the word *kiln*." Not very satisfying, but it works.

Jon stared at me for three seconds, then cried, "Missing LINK!" Of course. Get it? Not kiln, but link. Beautiful answer.

Look what happened. Individually, both of us had come to a conclusion. Both failed. But my half-baked idea—my "first pass" solution—brought thunder to the synapses of my brother's brain. My failure made possible *his* success. That makes it *our* success.

All deep or technical learning I do is cyclic. When I'm first learning a new skill or subject, I don't think of myself as ignorant, I think of myself as a "first-cycle expert" on the long but sure road to becoming a first-*class* expert. There is no end to cyclic learning. There's always a way to further refine what I know.

The *Obsess and Forget* Heuristic

Obsess and Forget is an alternation heuristic that works like this:

1. **Obsess.** Pounce on a subject like it was your first meal in months. Immerse yourself in it.
2. **Forget.** When your energy for that subject

wanes, allow yourself to let it go. Forget what you
learned.
3. **Repeat.**

I studied calculus when I was fifteen. I didn't enjoy solving calculus problems (they weren't authentic for me). I was more excited
about calculus concepts. With calculus I can figure the sum of an
infinitely long series of numbers. I love that idea! I've never needed
to do it, but it's nice to know I can. Except for one problem: long ago
I forgot how to do calculus.

There was a time when that depressed me. All that effort learning
something, just to have it slip away.

I am depressed no more. Using my peripheral wisdom, I look
forward to it. Forgetting has advantages:

- **Forgetting de-clutters my mind** and allows
  competing knowledge to come to the foreground.
  Sometimes I get wrapped up in details of a subject
  and feel bogged down. Forgetting can return my
  sense of mobility and make room for a competing
  obsession.
- **Forgetting helps clarify what matters.** I don't forget
  things all at once. I tend to forget useless things first,
  whereas the essential elements remain embedded in
  my mind. This improves my grasp of the subject, and
  prepares me to learn new details.
- **Forgetting gives me a critical distance.** Once I feel
  more distance from a subject, I can look at it dispas-

sionately and be a better judge of where I am and
what I need to learn next.

When forgetting happens, I remind myself that if I learned it
once, I can learn it again. I tell myself that everybody else forgets, too.
So, I'm not alone. And I've developed a library of reference materials
so that I can more quickly re-learn whatever I need.

THE *PLUNGE IN AND QUIT* HEURISTIC

In getting myself to read the *6502* book, I had stumbled into a technique for disarming the fear of being confused or overwhelmed. But
I hadn't realized it was a technique, yet. I couldn't have explained it,
even to myself. I couldn't use it systematically.

Today, it has a name: Plunge In and Quit. It's another heuristic
that harnesses the Principle of Alternation. It is a prime tactic of
cyclic learning.

Plunge In and Quit is a way of approaching any difficult task
when you don't know exactly how to do it or even if you *can* do it. It
consists of three parts:

1. **No promises.** Set aside any expectations about the
   outcome of what you're about to do.
2. **Tackle the hardest part, now!** Don't worry. Don't
   plan. Just jump in and do it.
3. **If it doesn't feel right, stop.** It's okay to quit. You
   made no promises, remember?

How different this is from the "don't start what you can't finish" attitude, or the "quitters never win" attitude!

Several examples of Plunge In and Quit in action:

The Recliner

My recliner broke. There was a lever on the side that made the leg rest come up and the back go down. I heard a snap inside the mechanism, and suddenly the lever hung freely, like a broken wing. My wife said "fix it." I explained that I am not a qualified recliner repairman. A week later, she said "fix it." I explained again that there were complicated gears and cables in there, like a Swiss watch. How would I know what to do? I'm in the computer software business. A month later she said "fix it." Finally, to show her, I flipped the recliner over and behold, there was the complicated mechanism, just as I had told her. But then I noticed a bracket dangling on the end of a cable. Next to it was an empty bracket-shape slot.

I felt like a monkey in one of those experiments with the banana on the string and a box nearby. Will the monkey push the box over and stand on it to get the banana?

I slid the bracket into the slot. Finished. Recliner repaired.

Elapsed time explaining why I would not be able to fix the mechanism: five weeks. Elapsed time once I tried to fix it: thirty seconds.

What was my error? As I confessed to my wife, I had committed what logicians call a *category error*. I had confused the ability to fix recliners in general with the ability to fix one particular problem with one particular recliner. Those are very different things. Before deciding

I couldn't fix it, I should have taken a few minutes to plunge in and try.
She thought my mistake was not following orders.

The Calculator

I once consulted at a company famous for its calculators. While I
was there, a fellow from another group asked me if I could take time
out to help him create a test strategy for his product. I didn't know
anything about his product, but told him sure, let's give it a shot. But
when we entered the conference room, I had no idea what his test
strategy should be. So I used a stalling tactic: *get the client talking*.
"Draw a picture of your product," I said, "and explain it to me."

He took up a pen. He opened his mouth. He began. Ten seconds
later I had my first test idea. I scribbled it down in my notebook,
trying to listen to him at the same time. After a few minutes, I was
overloaded with ideas. My writing hand began to cramp.

An hour later the conference room whiteboard was covered with
diagrams and notations. Between us, we had sketched a comprehensive strategy for testing the calculator. With his detailed knowledge
of the product, and my general knowledge of technology and testing,
the ideas poured forth.

I pretended as if I had known that would happen.

The Cell Phone Switching System

I often boast of the power of Plunge In and Quit. "Take me to your
software!" I tell clients. "Let me test it." One day I did this with a cell

phone switching system. I didn't know anything about such systems. I wasn't worried. They took me into their lab.

What wonders I beheld. It reminded me of Frankenstein's laboratory. Cabinet upon cabinet of obscure equipment. One whole wall was covered with tiny cell phones, connected to automated dialing software. They sat me at a console. I didn't know what I was looking at. I stalled by asking to see one of their test procedures. The first line of the procedure directed me to "Set the MSA to an RTT of 8."

After ten minutes I had to shrug. "This isn't working out. I suppose I will have to study the acronyms and features a bit more before I can just dive into the testing." You know, my clients don't mind when my plunging-in fails—it validates them. They hire me because they think they face difficult problems, after all. They are happy whether or not my tactics work, although for different reasons.

I always plunge in, sometimes I quit. It's okay to quit. That's why it's called "plunge in and *quit*."

THE *PROCRASTINATE AND PUSH* HEURISTIC

Now let's look at the opposite of plunging in: procrastination; Putting tasks off instead of doing them now.

It follows from the principles of Alternation and Peripheral Wisdom that procrastination is not necessarily a bad thing. For me, procrastination is a normal and necessary part of thinking and learning.

Procrastination is so misunderstood. Start from the beginning: it is only possible to procrastinate if there is a commitment to do something. A lot of what looks like procrastination is simply the refusal to accept responsibility. I didn't want to do my homework, so I didn't do it. That was not procrastination—that was rebellion.

Also, it can't be procrastination if there hasn't been an opportunity to complete the task. This happens when other tasks are more important. You don't blame a firefighter for leaving dirty dishes in the sink when the fire alarm goes off.

Procrastination occurs when I am committed to a task, I have the opportunity to do it, and yet instead I do something else that seems less important. I often procrastinate when I need to study, learn, write, or synthesize new ideas. I call that *creative* procrastination.

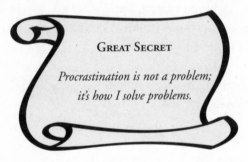

GREAT SECRET

Procrastination is not a problem;
it's how I solve problems.

The key to understanding creative procrastination is that much of creative work happens unconsciously. I may not be aware that I'm working or learning, even when I am. My mind is mysterious and mercurial, even to me. But I need a way to gently manage it. How do I remind it there's a deadline to meet?

Here's how. The Procrastinate and Push heuristic:

1. **Let myself sit for a while.** For a few days I don't try to think about the problem I must solve or the

work I must produce. However, I am open to spontaneous ideas, and I keep my notebook close by. It's like being in the dining room of my mind, chomping on breadsticks and waiting for the food. Meanwhile, pressure is growing to get the task done.

2. **Knock sharply at the kitchen door of my unconscious.** I get up and say, okay, I want to get this done. What ideas do I have? What do I need to do? I'm hungry! Let's go! If no thoughts come to me, or if they feel sluggish and dull, that indicates the good ideas are still cooking.

3. **If the door won't swing open, go back to step 1.** As deadline pressure builds, I knock harder and more frequently.

This heuristic is similar to Follow the Energy, and could also be called Pester the Energy.

Other heuristics work in concert with Procrastinate and Push:

Bold Boasts

To get myself going, I frequently promise to write an article or teach a class for a specific client at a specific time. I choose a task that is difficult, but not terribly difficult. For example, during one of the times I was having trouble writing this book, I promised to teach a one-day seminar on self-education. This "bold boast" would cause me to lose credibility if I didn't come through on it. As a result, I was motivated to create new materials. Some of them I used in this book. I find that for the magic to work, my bold boasts must be specific promises to specific people to do something by a specific time.

Graduated Deadlines

I wrote a dozen articles for *Computer* magazine one year, and never missed a deadline. The way I did this was by instructing the editor not to tell me the true deadline. I asked him what would be the most convenient deadline for him, and I tried in good faith to meet it. If I couldn't meet it, I would ask him for another week. If I blew that schedule, I'd ask to know the true Line Of The Dead. This helped me manage my energy. I didn't want to stay up all night to meet a fake deadline. But I also didn't want to force my editor to press without the article he was promised.

Springboard Procrastination

Sometimes when I go to knock on that kitchen door, someone kicks it from the other side, and I go flying back into the tables. I first noticed this when I was a kid, and Mom would tell me to clean my room. Instead of cleaning my room, I would have a sudden overpowering urge to read a book that I hadn't looked at in weeks. I found myself wondering, did she ask me to clean my room because she knew it was the perfect way to make me read this book? I discovered I could often use the energy of the procrastination impulse to get other things done. For instance, during the writing of this book, I successfully channeled the urge *not* to write into three months of exercise. I lost forty pounds.

Parallel Projects

Jerry Weinberg once told me his secret for writing one book a year: "I spend five years writing each book," he confided. "But I'm writing five books at once!" I do that, too. I have many projects and tasks going on. Books and journals are piled all over the office, all over everywhere. My email overflows. With so much going on, I can procrastinate on any one project, on *all* the projects, while still accomplishing a lot overall.

Downshifting

Sometimes my procrastination is because I have given myself too big of a job. So after I've been procrastinating and pushing for a while, I ratchet down my expectations. I lower my quality standard, or narrow the scope of the project. One way I do this is to say to myself, "I can always improve on it later." Another way is to shift my focus to one little piece of the work. For instance, to get through a tough part of writing this book, I spent several days just formatting the text to make it look pretty. Somehow that unjammed my mind and the writing got easier.

HOW ARE THESE HEURISTICS DIFFERENT?

The big heuristics I've discussed are mostly heuristics of alternation. They are useful because any difficult learning is a cyclic process. But they look similar, don't they? This is where Contrasting Ideas comes in. To clarify my methods, as I'm becoming aware of them, I ask myself: what is unique about each one? When I see those distinctions clearly, I am better able to appreciate each heuristic for what it offers.

Here's how I think they're different:

- **Plunge In and Quit** is a way of taking action without making a commitment. *It gets me going.*
- **Cyclic Learning** focuses on tolerating confusion, progressively working through it. *Once I am going, it helps me keep going.*
- **Follow the Energy** focuses on working with, not against, my feelings. *It helps me know where to go.*
- **Long Leash** focuses on the benefits of being distractible. *It helps me go where I didn't know I needed to go.*
- **Obsess and Forget** focuses on the benefits of letting go of knowledge as a way to obtain better knowledge. *It helps me feel good about stopping after I've been going for a while.*
- **Procrastinate and Push** focuses on honoring and supporting unconscious creative work. *It helps me feel good about being stopped, when I've already been stopped for a while.*

8

Emancipated Minor

I quit school and lived

"Unless you want to pump gas for money when you grow up, you better start taking your schoolwork more seriously," Mrs. Creveling told me in eighth grade. "Schoolwork may seem silly to you. You know what? It *is* silly sometimes. But if you play the game you'll have more opportunities in life."

"I'd rather not play that game," I replied. "I won't need money. I will live off the land in the Rocky Mountains. I'll build my own shelter. Hunt rabbits and tubers." I was serious. I'd been through hunter training camp. I spent a lot of time wandering the woods in Vermont.

The forest is real. That's what I loved about it. The forest doesn't play or pretend. Wilderness survival is the ultimate authentic problem.

But there was an important bit of truth in Mrs. Creveling's warning: society is organized to reward people who behave conventionally. Life is less convenient for those who chart their own course.

What Mrs. Creveling didn't want to tell me is that millions of unconventional people on our planet *do* make an honest living. Artists, writers, musicians, entrepreneurs. Yes, it's harder to tramp through the thorn bushes than to follow the paved road with everyone else, but it can be done.

Don't come out in public as a buccaneer if you're not willing to tramp through the thorn bushes . . .

LEAVING HOME AND SCHOOL

It certainly looked to be a thorny start for me. On September 28, 1980, I was evicted by my own parents. Mom sent me off to live in a motel room, a mile from the family home. I was allowed to return once a week to do my laundry.

I was fourteen, just starting high school.

She sent me away for a pretty good reason—I had threatened to kill my stepfather, Jon. It sounds more terrible than it was. He and I were shouting at each other about whether or not I was going to clean my room. I thought he was going to hit me, so I told him I would get my shotgun and shoot him if he did. He had never hit me before. I had never shot at anyone before. No damage was done, but it was too near a miss for Mom.

She made an arrangement with the manager of Mother's Motel, nearby, and Dad sent me child support checks each month to pay for necessities. After the cost of housing, I would have twenty-five dollars per week for food, and no money for anything else. I ate lots of canned soup.

A few days after our fight, just before I left, my stepfather talked to me in an encouraging man-to-man sort of way, telling me I could come home if I accepted the rules and chores that go with family life. I told him I understood. I was thinking, *I will never EVER come back here. Except to do laundry.*

Richard,

Sorry about all this. I was very quick to involve you in this crisis, when if I just thought for a few minutes I'd conclude you can't be much help, and it only makes you feel more helpless. I haven't talked to Jim since he talked to you, so I don't know his latest thoughts. But we can't live with tension and Jon and Jim threatening each other. Jon is bigger and I've given him the authority to call the shots. I may disagree with the intensity of his discipline on occasion, but it simply would not work if I overrode his decisions all the time.

I have investigated a motel-apartment nearby and they will rent to a minor if there's no trouble. It's $160 a month. Jim would have to walk about a quarter mile across the channel bridge to catch the school bus. I'll ask before I do anything, if he'd rather live with a family he knows, or live alone. Maybe even a month or two by *himself may make home look better to him. Actually, he likes it fine at home, if Jon would just leave him alone. Since he won't, leaving home is the only thing. I wish Jim was different. I wish Jon was different. I wish there was money for a private school. A lot of wishing won't make anything so.*

I'm sure there are a dozen ramifications of this move yet to be discovered and dealt with. I'm going to do my best to deal with them and not let the whole home be destroyed.

—Letter from Mom to Dad, September 1980

It sounds bad, but it was wonderful. I loved being alone. I felt free, just like being in the forest, only with more amenities. In my apartment, no one yelled at me. There were no unspoken, obscure social requirements I was expected to fulfill. A great weight lifted. The first night in my new place, I ate pizza while watching the first installment of Carl Sagan's *Cosmos* on public television.

My room was dilapidated but cozy, with running water and a twenty-year-old gas oven that almost killed me a few times when its pilot light went out and filled the room with fumes. I bought my groceries at The Harbor Store just a hundred yards away, and I caught the bus to school another few hundred yards beyond that. I had my computer and a black-and-white TV. Everything I needed.

Mother's Motel: My room was the last one on the left.

I no longer felt angry all the time. I learned how to manage money. I discovered I could live for weeks eating only pancakes. Then for weeks more, I lived on spaghetti. One month I ran out of cash and couldn't afford food for three days. I ate white sugar to stave off the hunger (it just made me sick). I would not repeat that mistake.

If you're having a hard time imagining a middle-class fourteen-year-old kid managing his own life without getting into drugs and being victimized by bad people, I understand. But, listen. This happened in rural, peaceful, safe, quiet Vermont years before terrorism and school shootings put people on edge. Hitchhiking was considered a safe activity for children. Most people didn't lock their doors. The major crime in our area was pranksters shooting transformers off of power lines or shooting deer out of season. The major cause of untimely death was falling through the ice of Lake Champlain. It was an innocent time in an innocent place.

Although it wasn't secret, not many people knew I lived alone. I just didn't have many friends to tell, and the few I had were harmless and bookish. Drugs were a problem somewhere, but not among anyone I knew. Those who might have corrupted me didn't like me enough to bother. I did get drunk, twice. Both times at a Dungeons & Dragons party with a bunch of other harmless wits.

I enjoyed alcohol, the few times I tried it. It made me dizzy. It was fun being dizzy. I would have done it more. But my sister heard about the drinking and told my father. He was on the phone to me immediately.

"James, you can get drunk all you like. It's up to you," he said. "You don't belong to me. You know that. But, still, I want you to know: I worry about you. I'm afraid you'll get into some terrible trouble. Would you consider staying away from alcohol?"

I was shocked to hear that Dad wanted something from me. Normally he didn't seem to care what I did as long as I was pursuing happiness.

"It's no big deal, Dad. It's just fun." I replied. Finally, here was some little thing *I* could do for *him*. "But if it makes you happy, I won't drink."

I didn't take a sip of alcohol for eight years, except for an anticlimactic visit to a bar on my twenty-first birthday. Dad's little nudge made a big difference. Today it's hard to remember that I once thought it was fun to get drunk. As Mr. Bedrin had, in sixth grade, my father talked to me as if I were an adult. Respect worked on me.

I got to know my father by telephone. During the winter of 1980, I'd huddle in the phone booth outside the Harbor store and call him. It was often well below freezing in the phone booth, but his voice was all warm encouragement, the only adult in my life who seemed to think I would amount to anything. No wonder. My father is a very impractical man. Almost the opposite of my stepfather, that way.

I wanted him to send me to a special school, somewhere. I'd heard about the Summerhill Institute in England, where all classes were optional. My older brother and sister had gone to Interlochen Arts Academy, and that sounded like an adventure, too. I dreamed of going to Caltech, someday, just because I'd read an article about its tradition of sophisticated practical jokes.

In the end it was a daydream. Dad couldn't send me anywhere. He had recently declared bankruptcy. The only thing he could do was talk. But he did that well. He wove spells with his voice. His usual technique was a Socratic interview. He might begin, "What do you most want to do in the world?" leading into a two-hour dialogue about things that matter and how to find them.

What I didn't want was to go to a school that offered nothing but drudge work served with sanctimony. Almost as soon as I left my mother's house for Mother's Motel, I became a serious truant. I missed almost thirty days of school over the course of the year. I discovered later that the school was sending notes home to Mom. She threw them into the garbage, unread.

As the year went on, my anxiety over school lapsed into distracted indifference. I felt like a ghost in the halls.

Then as summer vacation approached, I saw an article in *Time* magazine that kicked me in the stomach. It was called "Here Come the Microkids": all about computer-obsessed teenagers like me. But one in particular, Eugene Volokh, was going to college *and* working as a programmer, at the age of fourteen.

Hey! What about me? Why did he get to do that? What paperwork did his parents go through to make that happen? I still fantasized that I could skip the rest of high school and go directly to college. The only things stopping me were lack of money and no self-discipline. Plus I had no patience, no idea how to get around the normal rules for going to college, no notion of who to ask to help me do it. I was a terrible student on paper, then again also a terrible student *not* on paper. And of course I was allergic to most forms of authority.

So, I brooded, wandered around town, noodled with the software I built, played my Dungeons & Dragons, matched wits with my friends, and tried, pathetically, not to think about my bleak future.

Richard,

. . . One point: if Jim wants to excel in the scientific area, structured education is usually necessary because of the vast amount of knowledge to be covered—much like engineering. There is so much to know that is already known, before experimentation and innovation can take place. Jon cites daily examples at IBM, where one research department can work years on a project only to discover the research had been done by another IBM division at another site . . .

—Letter from Mom to Dad, 1980

"Why are you still bothering with those people?" asked my dad, hearing me rant yet again about high school. "You're just making trouble there. Quit school and take care of your own education."

"You think I should?"

"Absolutely!"

So, with my father's blessing, I dropped out. The decision to quit happened just as quickly as it is taking you to read these words. Twenty years later, I asked him how he was so confident I would succeed without finishing school. He looked surprised. "I don't remember telling you that," he said. "*I thought it was your idea.*"

ENTERING THE SOFTWARE BUSINESS

When I tell people I quit school, most are amazed that I was able to get work at major computer companies in Silicon Valley. They figure that I must have been lucky, or perhaps I had a relative in the industry who took pity on me and gave me a job.

Actually it wasn't hard getting into the software business. The reason is simple: I knew how to do something that needed doing, and I was cheap. Lots of companies want people with those qualities. And despite my mother's worries, in the computer industry it's possible to get the necessary skills without going to a school. Eugene Volokh got his computer science degree, but I discovered I didn't need one.

My first job was not auspicious. My older brother Rob rescued me from Vermont, helped me get a room, and negotiated a job for me in the town where he lived: Fairfield, Iowa. I worked for minimum wage at Walker's Office Supplies, selling computers and writing software to support their office equipment repair shop. I was very bad at selling. In the six months I worked there, no one bought a computer from me.

Dad urged me to start my own software company. He seemed convinced that success was both imminent and inevitable. I read his book *Jonathan Livingston Seagull.* (I'd read it many times before, but finally, at the age of fifteen, I understood it.) I wanted to apply its lessons. I read his book *Illusions,* where he describes using creative visualization to get what you want. I tried to use the mystical power of coincidences to help me find a place in the world.

My plan was easy to summarize: *get out and try stuff.*

One December day in 1982, stuff I wanted to try walked into Walker's. His name was Dale Disharoon. He ran a software company. I immediately tried and failed to sell him an Apple II. I was the "iron man" of failing to sell computers.

"Actually, I'm looking for a programmer," he said. "Do you know anyone who can program the Apple II?"

I replied eagerly. "Yes! Me."

"In Assembly Language? Show me." So, I did. In those days, I carried my programs around with me, just in case someone were to ask that question. On the spot, he offered me triple what I was making at the store ($10 per hour!) if I would come work for him as a contract video game programmer.

With my parents' permission I filed for a legal status of "emancipated minor" at the age of sixteen. This meant child labor laws no longer applied to me, and I could enter into binding contracts on my own.

That's the beginning of my career: January 1, 1983. On that day, I set up a card table in Dale's living room and began programming the games he conceived and designed.

Dale was a kindergarten teacher who had become disillusioned with the school system, himself. The personal computer revolution prompted him to try his fortune as an independent game designer, and he quickly found success. He hired me because he wanted to expand his operation without spending a lot of money.

There's a great secret here:

GREAT SECRET

*Few people out there want
exactly what I'm offering,
but a few is all I need.*

If I can find the one person in a hundred who will value what I am and pay for it, the other ninety-nine won't matter.

Dale taught me so much. How to behave like a professional, how to drive, how to negotiate a contract. He played the guitar, and insisted I learn an instrument, too. I went jogging with him three times a week.

I discovered that being paid to learn felt a lot better than being a schoolroom slave. I discovered pride in my work. Why did I accept direction from him when I would not accept it from my teachers at school? At first I thought it was because he paid me. Much later I realized it was something else, underneath the money: I respected him, and I wanted him to respect me. It was another echo of Mr. Bedrin.

That first year I wrote games with titles like *Hey Diddle Diddle, Alphabet Zoo,* and *Adventure Creator.* I also worked on the software examples for a book on programming (*Commodore 64 Puzzlements*). My games were sold in stores nationwide and advertised in magazines. COMPUTE!'s *Gazette* magazine even did a story about Dale and me as a programming duo. When Dale moved from Iowa to California, I followed him.

Several years later, my portfolio of games, my programming knowledge, and my naïve exuberance would convince a manager at Apple Computer to hire me. Five years had elapsed between dropping out of school in Vermont and joining the big leagues at Apple in California.

9

Guaranteed Not Stupid

How do I know I'm any good?

As a child I suffered from a terrible, wasting fear, one that had such a hold on me that I could not speak about it to anyone: *I was terrified of not being smart enough.* The fear sapped a lot of energy I otherwise might have put into my education. It made me pugnacious, but also easy to intimidate. If a subject looked difficult to study, I would put it out of my mind rather than confront the possibility that my gray matter was inadequate.

We hear about girls who believe they are too fat, no matter how they starve themselves. I was like that about my brain. I needed to be able to solve any problem with my mind and learn any skill. But my ambition to think far exceeded my ability. It tormented me. No level of intelligence was enough. Every failure of cleverness, knowledge, or memory was a humiliation. I didn't just want smarts, I wanted to be a prodigy. A hero brain.

The incandescent mind I craved did not appear, but still I had faith. I believed that I must have a *secret* talent. Yeah! I just didn't yet know what it was. Maybe the talent would be unleashed only by a particular activity. I searched for it. Maybe I'm a piano genius? Tried that—no. Inventions? My ideas fell apart. Maybe a math whiz? I was good at math, but not scary-good. Art? Not really. Writing? My fiction was self-indulgent junk. I tried chess, too. But for every game I won, I lost a hundred.

At seventeen, I tried to face my fear by taking an IQ test. But assigning a number to my brain did not help. Now instead of vaguely not smart enough, I felt *measurably* not smart enough.

I didn't like my score, but it was high enough to join Mensa, a social organization for people who are supposedly good at taking IQ tests. I thought I could conquer my inadequacy by challenging other Mensans. That also didn't help.

My first Mensa party was full of ordinary party banter. "Hey Paul, how's the car coming along? Have you tried the salsa?" "You think Reagan can be re-elected after invading Grenada?" Stuff like that.

"How do these Mensa meetings work?" I asked. I had expected to be hit with math problems or something. "Is there some kind of guided discussion?" I glanced around. It seemed like a normal cocktail party. The kind I hate because I never learned how to behave at parties, and I don't know how to talk about things that don't matter.

My host smiled over at me. "Oh nothing like that. It's just a get-together."

"But this is Mensa. We all took IQ tests to qualify . . ." I trailed off.

"A lot of people are in Mensa so they can socialize with other friendly people, not because they want to show off their intellect," she said gently.

"Really? I don't understand that. I came here to bash brains."

"You'll find, James, that there're all kinds of people in Mensa, and they have different reasons for joining. It's just a social club like any

122

other. A lot of these people don't think of themselves as Big Thinkers. There is only one thing you can say for *sure* about a Mensan."

"What's that?"

"We are guaranteed not stupid."

What a strangely low standard! They were friendly, though, so I kept going to the parties.

The crisis came one day when I was twenty. I read an article about the smartest person in the world. The article included some of her thoughts on philosophy, and I caught myself thinking, "What pompous nonsense. The woman's an idiot!"

The reply in my head was instantaneous: "Who are you to argue with her? An IQ test proves she's the smartest person in the world! You aren't qualified to dispute her words."

It's hard for me to describe what happened next. It was like being attacked by a swarm of bees, except each bee was a thought that stung my soul. I no longer knew my purpose. I no longer felt hope. I didn't know why I lived.

It was mid-afternoon. I put myself to bed.

I stayed in bed for three days. I had no appetite. Mostly, I slept. I don't remember much about my waking moments, except that the same useless thoughts looped and screeched through my aching head.

I could no longer deny my fear. I was no prodigy. No great genius. I had no secret super-talent. Indeed I was not smart enough to do things I once dreamed I would do. I would not be a great scientist, mathematician, or chess master. There would always be someone smarter who could do what I do better. The best I had to offer the world was only mediocre.

Why bother, then? Why do anything? No reason, except hunger and thirst. No reason that I could see.

But on the third day, as I lay there, like a ship dismasted, a pillow over my face, a new idea emerged. It appeared first as a question:

Q. *"What about dogs?"*
A. Memories of dogs. I saw dogs in my mind's eye. I love dogs. Then a dialogue unfolded in my head. Here it is as well as I can remember it:

Q. *"Are you worthless because you're not smart enough?"*
A. "Yes."

Q. *"Are you the stupidest person in the world?"*
A. "No."

Q. *"Therefore all people less smart than you are also worthless?"*
A. "Hmm. Maybe."

Q. *"You are in the top 1 percent of IQ. What about someone in the bottom 1 percent of IQ? Is that person completely worthless?"*
A. "Well, no. Not necessarily. There are other things people are good for other than problem-solving or speed reading."

Q. *"Like what?"*
A. "Love, I suppose."

Q. *"What about dogs? Dogs don't do Calculus, do they? But isn't it true that even a dog can show love? Even a puppy can. Surely a puppy is among the least educated of mammals, isn't it?"*
A. "Yes, puppies are savants of affection."

Q. "And love, affection, enthusiasm, loyalty, respect, service—all such things—they are available to all of us equally, aren't they? They have nothing to do with intelligence."
A. "That's true."

Q. "But how can these things be of value? How does that value manifest itself?"
A. "A person who receives love feels important. He feels real. He feels he can face life's trouble, because he doesn't face it alone. To love gives value to another life directly, immediately."

Q. "Do you have the ability to show love? Can you give the gift of your attention and encouragement to someone else? A dog can do it, can you?"
A. "Yes, I can."

Q. "So, if life is *not* a problem-solving competition—if life is a moment of miraculous light and warmth in an otherwise dark cold universe, and if any of us can project that nurturing idea—*are you worthless because you're not smart enough?*"

GREAT SECRET

Intelligence is just a tool.
Love is the point.

I felt reborn. It was my initiation ordeal.

Love is a word with a lot of baggage. But I think it's the right word. I'm talking about good feelings, feeling good as a person. Love comes from inspiration or intuition, rather than being a product of rational calculation.

From a loving perspective, life doesn't look like a battle, but more like a cooperative work of art, or a great feast. Anyone can contribute; everyone can benefit.

When I reinterpreted my own life in these terms, I began to see the motivation for much of my learning and most of my work as a programmer: I craved respect. In other words, love. Not excitement, freedom, or money.

I began to notice how the other people in my life were helping me. My family, my wife, my cat, my boss at work, my friends in Mensa. Even people who didn't know me had written things that encouraged or inspired me.

Then I understood how to handle people who were smarter than me: respect them for what they are; help them get what they need. By doing that, I become a part of their story. Instead of competing with them, I could join with them, or learn from them. But even if I competed, my competition could have a new purpose: to enrich my opponent, not just myself. I could treat competition as a special kind of collaboration.

The slogan of the local Mensa chapter, "guaranteed not stupid," now made sense. It was not a low standard. It was a way of saying that we don't know the significance of intelligence, we're not going to take it too seriously, and we're not going to let it divide us. I kept my Mensan friends after that, but no longer felt the need to be a member of an organization that sorts people by IQ.

LOVE AND PLUNDER

Buccaneering is an independent way of life. Yet the thought of service to others infused me with new self-worth. Is that a contradiction? No, because the independence of buccaneering is independence from *authority*, not from humanity. Although I make my own decisions about my education, I do that while appraising how I might be of better service to my friends, family, and colleagues.

In terms of the buccaneer metaphor, I sail and I plunder ideas. But what good would plunder be if I didn't sail home and share it with friends? As buccaneers, we can be humanitarians, too. We are humanitarians on our own terms.

SELF-APPRAISAL FOR BUCCANEERS

I suffered my little crisis at twenty because at that time I held an unworkable belief about what made life worth living. I had to find a new way of valuing myself.

If buccaneer-scholars wander zigzag paths of learning and distrust institutional credentials, then how do we evaluate ourselves? How do we know we are making progress? It took me a few years, but I found some answers. First, some principles:

- **My public status comes from my reputation, my portfolio, and how I do on life's tests.** Reputation is the story other people tell about me. My portfolio is the part of my work available for review. A test is

127

any opportunity to demonstrate my knowledge and skill.

- **My personal sense of worth comes mainly from feeling lovable.** I want people to like and respect me, but I don't need them to. Feeling lovable means that I think anyone would like and respect me as long as they were *not crazy* and they *truly knew me.*

- **My public and personal statuses are not necessarily aligned.** Either one can be in good condition while the other one is broken. I can have a high standing in my career or family, yet know that it is based on fraud. Or I can know that I'm terrific, yet work for an employer that doesn't want what I have to offer. For me, I feel terrible stress when my public reputation doesn't mirror my private sense of myself. I need to bring them into alignment. That can mean changing my job or my project.

- **My public status allows me to make a living. My personal sense of worth makes me want to live.** I earn my bread with my public status. Do people want to hire me? Are they interested in my ideas? But before I can put energy into my work, I first have to believe I'm personally worthy.

Here are some of the heuristics I use to evaluate myself. They work on a personal level as well as when I'm making a case to someone else, say, a potential employer.

1. Consider the second-order perspective.

A first-order perspective is the way things are. A second-order perspective means *how* they got that way and *how* they are going to be in the future.

I take a second-order perspective when I choose to think about how I'm learning, rather than beating myself up for not knowing a particular fact or not having a particular skill. If I'm not where I want to be, am I moving in the right direction? If I'm not moving in the right direction, am I at least trying to move in the right direction? (When I console myself with the second-order perspective, my thoughts often include the phrase "at least . . .")

When I was twelve, I experimented with higher-order perspectives by trying to make the most honest possible statement about my own honesty. I wanted to say that I always told the truth, but that didn't seem to be true, so I added qualifiers. Eventually, I constructed this formula:

> "I always tell the truth . . .
>
> and when I lie, at least I always lie in a way that does not hurt someone . . .
>
> and when I hurt someone with a lie, at least I always confess and ask forgiveness . . .
>
> and when I don't confess and ask forgiveness for hurting someone with a lie, at least I always suffer for it . . .
>
> and when I don't suffer for failing to confess for hurting someone with a lie, at least I know I was supposed to suffer."

Each clause of the statement steps outside the previous one, revealing it to be a partial truth, but by doing that, the whole thing seems to encompass more of the complexity of the situation. In a similar way, I can step outside of most situations and find a higher point of view that doesn't seem so bad.

This tactic helps me maintain my patience with a slow process of improvement. That may be why the second-order perspective is popular with politicians, who speak of measures that may not solve any problem but still "send a signal" or "move in the right direction."

2. Consider the contribution perspective.

The contribution perspective means looking at how other people are better off because of you—even if your own goals are not met. Remember George Bailey? He's the character played by Jimmy Stewart in the movie *It's a Wonderful Life*. In the film, Bailey is given the chance to see how the world would be if he had never lived. The experience helps him see the value of his life, even though he never pursued any great dream or heroic venture. With the help of an angel, he discovers that hundreds of people are living better lives because of his many small kindnesses and services.

I wonder whom we have to thank for smiling at Einstein while he was working on his Theory of General Relativity? It was a terrible struggle. He must have been depressed now and then during the years he worked on it. Someone brought him lunch. Probably his wife, Elsa. And his stepdaughter Margot helped manage his affairs, later in life. I wonder if Einstein had a dog, too? I bet lots of people contributed to Einstein's success.

I especially think this way because my own wife takes care of the paperwork for our consulting business, so that I can focus on the part I'm good at: daydreaming and talking. Come to think of it, the existence of this book is largely due to my family keeping the distractions away during the months I was brooding, procrastinating, then finally putting words to paper.

The first time I can remember taking the contribution perspective was when I was thirteen, chopping wood in the rain in the middle of the wilderness. My hiking buddies were in the tent, dry and comfortable, playing cards. I was soaking and shivering, splitting the kindling so I could start a cooking fire. It was my turn to do this chore. On previous days when it had been my turn, I groaned my way through it. This time something was different: I felt happy. That had never happened before. Although I felt cold and uncomfortable, hearing my friends enjoy their game changed my focus. My work was contributing to them, and I was part of them, and suddenly I felt as though their pleasure was my own. It was a powerful moment, and I think back on it whenever I'm doing a boring or dirty chore around the house.

If I see myself as part of a community, I can also gain comfort from the *unique* contributions I make. This is what I call the "elliptical team." Let me explain. In any group of people working together, different people will have different abilities. We might picture these abilities as lines fanning out from a single point, each line being a different ability. The distance from the central point on any one line is how much of that ability someone has.

131

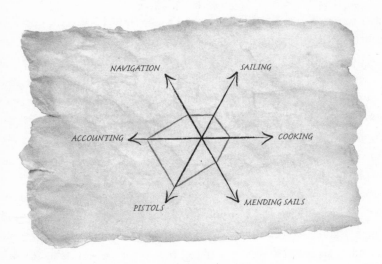

Now imagine connecting the dots of each ability to form a closed shape, as in the diagram. (This is sometimes called a "radar" or "kiviat" chart.) In this example, the buccaneer is better at pistols than he is at cooking.

Early in my career as a test manager I thought it was a good idea for everyone in my team to be good at every ability. When this idea was plotted on a kiviat chart, it was as if everyone was supposed to be a "circle." But I discovered that doesn't work well. People have different talents and interests; they won't be equally good at everything. More importantly I found that a team of people with different abilities works better together, because each person contributes something unique and is appreciated for that contribution. This leads to more collaboration than competition.

When I say "elliptical team," I imagine that each member of the team is like an ellipse tilted at a different angle—strong in some ways, weak in other ways. This image helps me simultaneously appreciate the power of the team and of each individual on the team.

AN "ELLIPTICAL" TEAM

TOM

HARRY

DICK

EVERYONE IS BETTER AT SOMETHING

The contribution perspective can be combined with the second-order perspective. First-order contribution is doing something for somebody. Second-order contribution is helping someone do something *better* than they otherwise could. Even if I'm on a team and there's nothing I am best at, I can still help the best get more done or feel great about doing it.

Even when I'm competing, I can take the contribution perspective. Have you ever seen one of those sports movies that ends in The Big Game? The lovable loser baseball team, for instance, might get a home run in the bottom of the ninth inning. Hurray for them. But when I see that, I keep thinking about the pitcher who just blew the game. Does he know that he's in a movie, and the movie was about the other team? When someone wins the Big Game, someone else must lose.

So one day, while losing another game of chess, I realized I'm just like the villain in one of those films. I'm the guy who loses. Then I saw that if I played hard and lost, I would be giving the gift of winning to my opponent. I could enjoy that experience exactly as if I were a member of the audience watching the movie. Hurray for you, you beat the bad guy, who was played by me! You're welcome!

Ever since then I have not minded losing.

3. Separate aspirations and expectations.

My expectations for myself are what I *know* I can do. My aspirations are what I *hope* I can do. If I fail to meet my own expectations, something is wrong. Something is broken. My aspirations must always exceed my expectations. Otherwise I self-destruct. Therefore my expectations define what being healthy and normal means to me.

That means my expectations should be low! The lower they are, the easier it is to feel healthy and normal.

Consider the diagram. Imagine that it is the side view of a container that can hold my level of talent, skill, achievement, or "goodness" in some area. For example, say that it represents my ability to play chess. The lower dashed line is my level of expectation. The upper line is my level of aspiration. If I fill this container with my chess ability, which lines will it reach? If I'm really bad at chess, it may not even reach the first line. I will feel like a chess idiot. I will be worried and probably discouraged. I better lower my expectations. If I am good enough at chess to meet my expectations, then I will feel pretty good. I will continue to practice my chess playing. On the other hand, if I'm so good at chess that I exceed even my aspirations, then I will become bored with chess, and look for new adventures elsewhere.

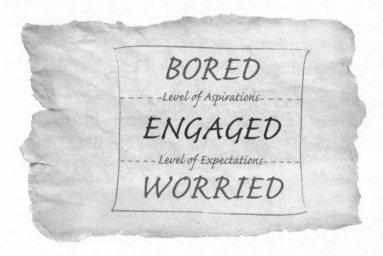

BORED

- - - Level of Aspirations - - - -

ENGAGED

- - - - Level of Expectations - - - - -

WORRIED

My aspirations should not be set at the same level as my expectations, because then there is no zone of engagement. I won't learn and grow, except by accident. If I set my aspirations very high, I have something inspiring to reach for, and if at the same time my expectations are low, I won't lose heart.

The mistake I made in my childhood was to have high aspirations but also to have expectations set at the same outrageous level. That meant I always felt inadequate. There was no middle place where I could exceed what I needed to do while going after something I hoped I could do.

The Ping-Pong Paradox

Some years ago my brother Jon and I were learning to play Ping-Pong, we noticed that competing with each other spurred us to try our best. Competition created intensity. But we also noticed that competing sometimes made us avoid experimenting with new moves. When you bring your "A-game," your "B-game" doesn't get much exercise. This is a paradox of competition: it helps you learn in some ways and it discourages learning in others. The way out of the paradox is through alternation: compete sometimes, and sometimes stop competing and just try something risky and unconventional.

The Ping-Pong Paradox illustrates expectations and aspirations at work. I won't jump toward an aspiration (learning a new spin serve in Ping-Pong, for instance) if I'm worried that I will fall short of an expectation (I might lose the game).

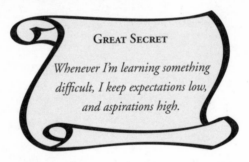

Great Secret

Whenever I'm learning something difficult, I keep expectations low, and aspirations high.

The Sail Power Principle

I learn the most from a situation when I must struggle to solve a problem, but not struggle *too much*.

This is important when sailing, so listen up, buccaneers. A sail with no wind won't move the ship at all. A sail with too much wind will tear the ship apart. Setting the sails and steering a course by the wind is like saying to myself, "I want to learn this," and establishing my expectations and aspirations. The wind itself is knowledge and experience whipping by me. Managing the tension in my sails is critical to getting good progress without damaging my ship. If my expectations are too high, that's like setting too much sail. But if my aspirations are too low, then I won't set much sail at all, and won't learn very much. So intellectual engagement comes *between* expectation and aspiration.

THE SAIL POWER PRINCIPLE

NO PRESSURE
NO PROGRESS

HEALTHY PRESSURE
GETTING SOMEWHERE

TOO MUCH PRESSURE
NO PROGRESS

Example: Shredded sails in fifth grade

In 1977 my school held a science fair. I chose computers as my topic. I knew almost nothing about computers. I didn't have access to a computer. I'd never seen a computer. I played with my mom's handheld calculator and I looked up computers in the encyclopedia. I thought I might build a computer, but my dreams far exceeded my ten-year-old kid's ability to create and execute a coherent and practical plan.

137

I expected myself to be able to write a respectable report about computers, at least, but even this proved too difficult. My expectations were too high. I suffered terrible writer's block. I felt that I didn't know anything worth writing down. I struggled for several weeks, feeling guilty and stupid. Then I realized I didn't know how to write a report of any kind, and I didn't know how to ask for help. I must have been sick on the day the rest of the kids were told how to do it.

In schools, turning in bad work is usually preferable to turning in nothing. Add that to the list of problems with schools. In order to turn in something, I resorted to a kind of fraud: the ancient schoolboy tactic of padding. Take a look at a paragraph from that report. You'll see what I mean. It's vapid, inauthentic, and I had no conviction, even as I wrote it. The truth was that I had failed to learn about computers, but I believed it was unacceptable to admit that.

> A computer is easily operated if computer principles are understood and the program completely comprehended. Unless you programmed the computer, it usually takes a college education. To program a simple computer, I've found, is a very hard mathematical process using various codes. The operation of a computer concerns pushing various buttons to equal question. But it all depends on the type of computer being operated.

I had such high expectations yet fell so short that turning in the report was an experience of pure humiliation. Even worse: the teacher gave me an "A" on it.

This is an example of a shredded sails situation. Broken rigging. The effect of struggling and failing on this task was to crush my confidence, because my expectations were set too high. That I received a good grade only taught me contempt for the grading system. For the rest of my school career, I avoided writing almost entirely. Ten years passed before I overcame my fear of writing.

I've since read reports that were just as empty as my fifth-grade prose, except they were written by adults. Maybe I wasn't the only one who got good grades for bad work. Lots of people seem to believe that turning in bad work is better than turning in nothing.

A good teacher—or a good manager—helps manage expectations of their students and workers to keep them motivated. We buccaneers must learn to do this for ourselves.

4. Co-opt the critics.

It's hard to take criticism, yet I need it to improve. Part of assessing myself is assertively rooting out my mistakes and weaknesses. Here are several ways I make criticism easier to take:

- **I try to be the first to cast stones at myself.** Criticism hurts less when it's no surprise. As I appraise my progress, I try hard to be the first person to know my faults. Then when someone else points at them, I can take the second-order perspective and say, "At least

139

I'm wise enough to know that already." Also, I take the second-order perspective by trying to be the first to acknowledge that when things are going well it may have been a fluke. *Don't be complacent, James!*

- **I know that criticism of me isn't necessarily my problem.** All criticism is relative to the worldview and values of the critic. The critic may have a personal grudge he's exercising. It might not even be a grudge with me, but someone who looks like me. Or maybe the guy is having a bad day. I don't know. When I'm at my best, I look at my critics and try to think how I could accept their criticism in a way that will make them feel good. Being an object of criticism is, from a contribution perspective, a service I offer to the critics. A critic I serve well, in this way, often becomes a friend.

- **I cultivate critics I trust.** When I have mustard on my chin, it's no embarrassment when my wife tells me. It's her duty. She wants me to look good. When I get criticism from someone I believe wants what's best for me, it's a lot easier to listen to. Over time, I collect people who will tell me things I don't want to hear, and do it because they want to see me do well.

- **Taking criticism well makes me feel tough.** If being a buccaneer means anything, it ought to mean I can look the scary truth in the face and smile. While I'm listening to someone tell me I'm not good enough, I remind myself that this process is the way I achieve deep self-respect. From that point of view, criticism is a gift.

There is a childish part of me that feels wounded by any kind of criticism. But I learned a little trick from one of my mentors, Jerry Weinberg, about how to deal with it: I notice the feeling and say to myself, "Oh, that's the childish part of me, again, doing what it likes to do. Funny little critter. It will settle down again, soon." This thought works almost like a calming spell. It helps me put that peevish, defensive feeling at arm's length, rather than having it burn inside me like a fire in a hollow tree.

5. Don't let numbers intimidate you.

Some people love statistics, test scores, game scores, anything that's easily quantified. This may be self-interest: people who happen to be good at taking exams are likely to think an exam score is great; people responsible for assessing lots of other people may also like an exam score, because it's easy and it looks fair. Numbers look scientific; and science is fashionable.

But every quantitative measurement is supported by a mass of beliefs and assumptions that no one puts numbers to. No one *can*. These are the *qualitative* judgments about what matters, what doesn't, and why. Qualitative decisions define the rules of the assessment games we play.

When I want to know if I'm any good, or if I want to demonstrate my worth to someone else, I look at the whole picture. I don't stop with a handful of simplistic measurements.

Sometimes other people define the rules by which I am judged, but I often can influence those rules. I do that by explaining how I might be useful or valuable in some way the judges haven't yet considered. This happens on a regular basis when I convince a client to hire me.

I get to choose how to interpret measurements and scores. I also get to choose what game I play. If I want to be a chess champion, then I'm stuck with chess rules. But in life there are a million different games. I move toward the ones that fit me. For instance, I'm attracted to software testing as a job because testing problems have no fixed solution. Every testing problem is a learning challenge. Testing always seems fresh to me, and it rewards ingenuity. It's a game where the rules are sometimes murky and mysterious, and for me, that's part of its charm. Perhaps the secret to happiness is finding the games we love to play, instead of learning how to win at games we hate.

Example: Speed Reading

Is faster reading better than slow reading? Seems like it would be. But reading speed is not the whole picture.

Imagine bursting through the door of a dinner party at a friend's house, rushing about pumping hands, and collecting business cards. Stop to pour a gallon of punch over your face, glug glug; tip a tray of pastries into your pants; then race outside again. Call it "speed partying," but it misses the point, even if you were to come out of there with some cards and the memory of a few new (alarmed) faces.

I once had goals like "read Toynbee's *Study of History*" or "read *Encyclopedia Britannica*." I thought that learning to read very quickly would help in achieving those goals. Then I tried a speed reading course. The most important thing I learned from it was how nice it is to read slowly. I get pleasure and power from slowness.

Having read something, in the sense of having dragged my eyes over text and memorized it, just gives me an empty feeling. I need a *relationship* with valuable ideas, not just a memory.

Now I understand that I have two reading speeds: scouting speed and mulling speed. Mulling speed is anywhere from zero to three hundred words per minute (It's zero if I'm staring at a diagram, or chewing over something I read yesterday). Scouting speed can be as fast as riffling through a book looking for pictures and headings (two pages per second), or as slow as six hundred words per minute.

When I'm scouting, I'm just trying to understand what material is there, without stopping much to absorb the details. Scout reading can benefit from speed reading techniques. But when I'm mulling, I'm finding connections between this text, other text, pictures, and the rest of my life. I'm interpreting and reinterpreting the book. I'm arguing with the author as I go. Reading is not just a game of memorization, for me.

That's what I mean by looking at the whole picture, and not letting numbers seduce you into a narrow view. Back when I thought the point of reading was to stuff as many facts in my head as possible in a unit of time, I was ignoring a lot of important stuff.

6. Celebrate the triumphs.

I celebrate by recalling stories of past achievements. I keep track of cool things I've learned, or tried to learn. I recite them silently to myself, once in a while.

I also recite them out loud, at times. Since I don't have a trophy room, and I can't wave at a wall full of paper certificates, I tell stories to establish my credentials as a thinker. I talk about specific things, such as how I learned to fly, program computers, or play harmonica.

Triumphs don't have to be big. Here's an example: years ago, I memorized 103 digits of the value of pi as part of a goofy competition with one of my schoolmates. Even today, I will spit out the first 41 of those digits at the flimsiest invitation (314159265 35897932384626433832795028841971! Honest, I didn't look it up!).

Memorizing digits of pi has not measurably improved my ability to calculate the circumference of the circles I encounter in my daily life. But it has improved my life. It is one more stout brick in the rampart of my self-respect. I recite digits of pi and I think to myself that I am a reasonably clever and valuable person. Don't get me wrong. Being able to recite those digits doesn't mean that I really *am* clever or valuable. I know that, but even so—I think of that little triumph and I feel good.

These stories give me emotional ballast, even if I don't tell them out loud. It's remarkable how certain moments from my past pop back into my mind at strange moments to give me comfort. Example: on July 4, 1986, I was walking along an embankment in a park, on my way to a cookout. Suddenly there was a ruckus up the hill, and I saw a child on a bicycle coming down toward me. He couldn't stop his bike. To my left was the top of a concrete wall and a-four foot drop onto sharp boulders in a culvert, below. To my right was the kid skidding toward the drop-off. His mother was charging after him but would not reach him in time. I reached out and grabbed him before he fell off the cliff.

His mother thanked me and they bustled away. Ever since, I've wondered, did I save him from a terrible head injury? Probably. My mind turns to that incident once in a while and I say to myself, "Well, at least I saved a kid, once."

When I tell this story it helps me remember another lesson: the most wonderful thing I do in my entire life may happen in the next ten seconds.

7. Celebrate the failures.

I have my revenge on failure whenever I can turn a failure into something useful. Here are some of the ways I do it:

- **Failure is funny.** First aid when I fail at something is to douse it with humor. Humor is my emotional fire extinguisher. Sometimes this is difficult when the disappointment of failing is fresh. Usually it takes a few days. For something embarrassing, like, oh, carelessly insulting the entire Apple Computer Fremont manufacturing facility during a tour by repeatedly making comments about how the assembly line workers looked like they were chained to their work (just to name something that may have happened to a guy named Schmames Schmach), it may take a few days to get through the mortification stage and find the cosmic joke.
- **It's vivid data.** I learn from whatever happens. There is no denying me. No matter what the disaster may be, I will learn. And hearing about other people's

trouble is such a pale experience compared with a firsthand, headfirst meltdown.

- **It sweetens success.** Think of failure as a sort of karma. I may try and fail, but in failing I've paid some dues. I've made an investment. When success comes I will feel all the more like I deserve it.
- **It's a teaching story I can sell.** The thing I love about screwing up is the knowledge that someday I will sell the story of my screw-up to a paying customer. I'll write about it, or I'll use it in a seminar. It's the sweetest revenge of all on the Fates: to brighten someone else's day or help them see the world a little more clearly by having them re-live a bit of my past misbehavior.

Reputation, Tests, and Portfolio

No buccaneer of old had a "Bachelor of Arts in Privateering" degree. There was no certification process. Buccaneer leaders gained reputation through the tests they faced in their work, and their portfolio of tangible outcomes. That's a clinical way of saying that sailors crowed about their exploits while getting drunk on their stolen and looted ships. Crowing, exploits, and loot equals reputation, tests, and portfolio.

I do the same thing. By writing articles and teaching classes, I'm able to show my work. I also have a website and a blog. I wrote a book. Most of the work I do for paying clients is confidential, but sometimes I have more easygoing employers who let me show off specific documents or programs I've written for them. That's my portfolio.

Then there are tests. When I stand and speak at a conference, when I solve a problem at work, or when I'm working with specific people, these are all tests. It isn't enough to have a portfolio of work; it must be good work. It must impress.

My portfolio and my performance on tests slowly gain a reputation for me. It's my reputation that brings customers from all over the world. I don't directly control my reputation. By holding strong opinions, I have gained both friends and enemies. On the Internet, with blogs, forums and social networking websites, a reputation can be made almost instantly.

Since I write articles and a blog, what I say is subject to commentary by anyone, anywhere, anytime. Much of what people say about my ideas is wrong, but I learned to live with that. Buccaneers work and thrive in the economy of ideas, and each of us can be our own brand name.

GREAT SECRET

*To build my brand name,
I must stand for something,
even if many people won't get it
or don't like it.*

My advice to new buccaneers is to exhibit as much of your work as possible. This is very easily done now on the Internet. Post examples of your work online. Participate in online forums and networking sites. Write a blog. For everything you post, remember that your enemies as well as your friends will read it. Just keep improving and expanding your portfolio. If it's good work, your reputation will quickly grow. If it's bad work—or good work that is too far ahead of its time—you will be ignored. Both of those problems are fixable.

Take pride in what you are.

10

No Prey, No Pay

Buccaneering at work

Ihave no discipline. Oh, you can point to things I've done that look like hard work. I shrug. That's not discipline, that's passion. Passion is a mysterious force that comes and goes, a restless breeze. Let me put it this way: if I have discipline, I certainly can't depend on it to get stuff done.

By the end of 1986, I was tired of programming computers. Not just tired, sick. Dale had given me several months of work to do and left town on a sabbatical. I was working alone now. But I found I could no longer do the job. My mind was balking again. It was the same feeling I'd once had about seventh-grade homework. The moment I sat down to write software, a wave of nausea would come over me and my mind would go blank. Burnout. Runaway mind, part two.

Instead, I spent a lot of time in coffee shops, writing self-absorbed poetry and social commentary in my notebooks. I also haunted the wonderful library at Chico State (500,000 books!), poking gingerly at books on education and philosophy. I started an online forum for philosophical debate, spending many hours crafting and responding to outrageous rhetorical attacks. I played a lot of Scrabble.

While I was struggling with my problem, the game industry was going through a shake-out. A lot of small companies were folding. By the end of the year, Dale came back from his vacation and shut down his business.

So, in May of 1987, nearing my twenty-first birthday, I was down to my last hundred dollars, and the only marketable skill I had was for something I could no longer force myself to do.

Then a recruiter called. She'd found a résumé I had sent months before. Would I like a job in Silicon Valley?

"I thought the industry had taken a downturn. Aren't there programmers starving in the streets of Sunnyvale?"

No, actually there's lots of work available. Would I like a job at Apple Computer, for instance?

"Sounds wonderful. What kind of work is it?" All feelings of burn-out were instantly replaced by a blazing electric neon YES in my heart. Apple Computer needs me. *Needs* me. I am being called to service.

The job was managing a team of testers.

"What do you mean, testers?" I asked the telephone.

The recruiter explained that testers examine a product someone else has created and find problems in it.

"They *pay* people to do that?" Interesting. I'd always tested my own work. Then again, I'd never worked on a team with more than two other people. In terms of the software industry, I was a crazy-eyed mountain man.

The idea of software testing intrigued me. Instead of pounding in rivets, I could sit comfortably under a parasol, judging other people's rivets. I could use my programming skills without actually having to program anything. It sounded like fun.

Management attracted me, too. I had never done it before, nor even seen anyone do it, but it sounded like being in command. I love being in command. James the tester. King James, testing *manager*. Sounded good.

I knew I'd better learn management, fast. On the way to Apple I bought a copy of *The One-Minute Manager*. It looked thin enough for rapid learning. I skimmed it as well as I could in the hour before the interview.

Walking into Apple may have been the first time I ever set foot inside an office building. First time seeing cubicles and conference rooms. First time seeing a carnival-sized cart of free hot popcorn parked in a hallway. Imagine working near the smell of melted butter! (Your eyes sting and you come to hate the smell of butter, it turns out.)

I'd been worried about my clothes. I didn't own a suit. But looking around, I fit right in. Everyone was dressed like me.

Two guys in a conference room asked me questions. I answered them and showed the portfolio of games I'd worked on. When they asked me about management, I repeated some of what I'd read in *The One-Minute Manager*. When they asked me about testing, I said what every programmer says: "I've tested my own stuff." It's not a good answer, but I didn't know that. Neither did they. No one in that room knew much about software testing. There are no university degrees in it. It's one of many new crafts that have emerged along with modern technology.

New industries are perfect for a buccaneering mind. The testing field was as wild and wide open as the Spanish Main ever was. When employers don't know what they need, what they need are people who are good improvisers.

After the interview, I went outside and walked twice around the building. This is where I belong, I thought. I will rock this place. Please please please hire me.

A couple of days later, they did.

I discovered that there had been only one other candidate for the position, and he was considered over-qualified (that means they didn't want to pay him what he was worth). But the main reason I got the job was that I charmed the hiring manager, and convinced him I would learn the job quickly. He wanted someone he could mentor, and I overflowed with enthusiasm to be mentored.

If my education is like a sea voyage, then the part that came before Apple was like paddling around the harbor. At Apple Computer my education truly set sail.

THE THRILL OF BEING NEEDED

My fatigue and nausea disappeared the moment I heard about the job. There was no healing or transition process. It was instantaneous. This taught me about the cause of burnout: when I don't feel useful and respected, I wilt like old lettuce. At Dale's company, I had worked alone most of the time. In school, I had also worked alone. I now think loneliness had been starving me.

Before Apple, I would have described myself as basically lazy. But before Apple, I had not been a valuable member of a team. I would discover, in the years that followed, that I am capable of cheerfully working eighty-five-hour workweeks, as long as I feel useful and respected by the people around me. I have to *feel* it, not just think it. The people around me help me feel it. My mind thrives on that human contact. It's honey. It's psychic fuel.

No longer becalmed, I had found the trade winds: they were blowing at the Research and Development division of Apple Computer.

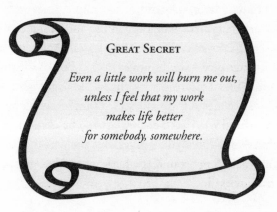

GREAT SECRET

Even a little work will burn me out,
unless I feel that my work
makes life better
for somebody, somewhere.

This has everything to do with educating myself. My motivation to learn is grounded mostly in being of service to my friends, family, coworkers, and all my clients (including anyone who may read what I write). I need to feel the connection between studying and people who matter to me. I felt that connection at Apple, where I was needed, but not at school.

Why the difference? If social life is so important to me, why do I argue with authority figures and challenge the systems around me? Shouldn't I be much less a fighter and much more eager to please? The answer is that I like running with a pack, but not following a herd. There's a big difference. Herd animals just go with the flow.

But in a hunting pack, independence and teamwork go together. The original buccaneers operated that way, too.

Catching the College Kids

I was a nervous man on my first day at Apple. At twenty, I was the youngest manager in the building. In all the gatherings and reorganizations we went through during the four years I worked there, I never met a younger manager. I was younger than many of the interns.

Also, I was a contractor. That meant Apple could fire me without notice or severance. I had little money and no credit.

The worst thing was that nearly everyone around me had a university degree. A good many had graduate degrees.

I had to catch up to the college kids. I brooded on it every day. I came to work with desperate fire in my soul to learn. Learn everything. Learn it now.

I began by scouting. The learning resources at Apple were overwhelming. I felt giddy. There were classes I could take. Visiting scholars gave seminars in the building. Our corporate fileservers were crammed with technical documentation.

The San Jose area (also known as the South Bay, Silicon Valley, or simply The Valley) is home to fabulous bookstores. And in those days Apple Computer had one of the best corporate libraries in the industry, fully staffed with reference librarians who—just like me—wanted to justify themselves through service.

As a manager, I supervised five testers, but no one closely supervised me. My boss, Chris, was in meetings most of the time. He needed me to get on with the work as best I could. This meant I could sneak away and read. I spent part of each afternoon in a donut shop across the street from my building, studying without interruption.

Chris was supportive. "You should not just read about software," he suggested. "Try to find solutions to our problems in other disciplines." Maybe Chris was more supportive than he ever knew. I treated that one casual suggestion as permission to spend work time to learn *anything*. I browsed many of the two hundred or so academic journals that came through the library. Even crazy stuff. I read "Anthropometry of Algerian Women," and "Optimum Handle Height for a Push-Pull Type Manually-Operated Dryland Weeder."

Of course I read every testing book I could find. I discovered software testing standards and studied those, too. I studied most evenings and weekends.

At first I thought I would learn a lot from the other testers. There were more than four hundred of them in my building. But talking to them revealed a startling truth: *nobody cared.*

Almost nobody. In the first six months I worked at Apple, out of all the testers in the software testing division, I met maybe ten who were also reading testing books. The rest muddled through without much ambition to master their craft. It was clear that catching the college kids would not be difficult, after all.

GREAT SECRET

Most people, most of the time, don't try very hard.

The pattern I experienced at Apple would be confirmed almost everywhere I travelled in the computer industry: most people have put themselves on intellectual autopilot. Most don't study on their *own* initiative, but only when they are forced to do so. Even when they study, they choose to study the obvious and conventional subjects. This has the effect of making them more alike instead of more unique. It's an educational herd mentality.

I talked to coworkers who wanted to further their education, but they typically spoke in terms of getting a new piece of paper, such as a bachelor's degree, a master's, or a PhD. For them, education was about the doors they believed would open because of how they were *labeled by institutions,* not about making themselves truly better as thinkers. Buccaneers, on the other hand, don't take labels too seriously. A buccaneer studies in the hope of unlocking Great Secrets! Wonder! Mastery! A buccaneer lives for the excitement of deciphering the mysteries of human experience. A buccaneer wants status, too, but only if that status is justly earned and sustained through the quality of his work.

I wanted to do good work at Apple. I burned with desire to feel useful. I resolved to become *expert* at my craft. I believed if I achieved that, wealth and status would follow. Labels like "master's degree in computer science" held no appeal for me. It dawned on me that success is not about what you know, it's about what you can discover and create. It's not about what you are, but about what you are *becoming* and what you can *cause to happen.* It's about learning, what I call intellectual buccaneering. I would create my own success by creating my own education. I would win reputation on the basis of merit rather than ceremony. That's the buccaneer way.

Not only could I compete in the software testing industry without the labels of formal schooling, *I could rise to the top of the field.* My competitive advantages were:

- A habit of self-education (due to the need to survive)
- Eagerness to question traditional ideas (due to my distrust of authority, lack of discipline, and desire to live authentically)
- The diversity of my studies (due to my restless attention span)
- Ambition (flaring up, now, because I felt needed)

This is a truth I couldn't have known in elementary school, nor in high school, back in Vermont. I wouldn't have seen it working at the office supply store in Iowa, nor in Dale Disharoon's garage in the little town of Chico. But here the truth was undeniable. Here I was surrounded by hundreds of engineers doing knowledge work in the heart of Silicon Valley, the cream of the industry, and I was doing fine! That's when I understood: *what I thought were my weaknesses were actually my strengths!* I could not succeed within the structure of formal schooling, but that very independence would lead me to excel in the "real world."

My Learning *Is* My Work

In the previous paragraph, I mentioned knowledge work. Let's talk about that.

Knowledge work means conceiving, developing, analyzing, studying, testing, packaging, communicating, selling, or buying the products of the human mind. In short it's all about *ideas*. Ideas are merely patterns. An idea has no intrinsic substance or value. But for knowledge workers, the right idea at the right time will lead to success, wealth, and happiness.

Knowledge work is a huge part of the modern economy. That includes science, engineering, medicine, law, politics, finance, journalism, marketing, technology, arts (literary, graphic, or performing), any kind of consulting or academics, and countless other occupations.

Any job or task can be turned into knowledge work. It's all in how you approach it. The artist Andy Goldsworthy is a good example. His art consists of arranging natural objects, such as sticks, stones, leaves, and icicles. Although he began as a farm laborer, and sometimes compares his work to picking potatoes, the truth is he's a buccaneer working in a unique way with profound ideas.

Knowledge work can be hard to manage, and companies are often tempted to over-manage it by establishing elaborate rules, tools, and processes that hobble creativity. But consistently successful companies don't try to mechanize or dictate thinking. Instead they create an environment that supports and encourages experimentation and problem-solving. I was fortunate to have a string of managers who did that for me. If I'd had more teachers doing that for me, I might have stayed in school.

Knowledge workers create intellectual property that pleases their customers. (In my case I produce advice, observations, analysis, reference documentation, training, coaching, and sometimes software.) They may deliver those products in writing, in person, or embedded in other products.

Knowledge workers face a big problem: overload. The mountain of useful things to know keeps growing. There is too much to be learned, and too many useful skills to be mastered. Not only is there a lot of it, but it all changes so quickly. *Nobody* can cram more than a little bit of it into their heads, and even that may soon be obsolete. Meanwhile, university training is a short, fixed period of education, often cut off from industrial practice. It's hard to see how university training could possibly be the solution to the education problem faced by today's knowledge workers.

That works out great for buccaneers! The historical buccaneers were successful because national navies couldn't cope with the challenge of patrolling the Caribbean and the South Seas. Modern buccaneer-scholars are successful partly because modern universities can't provide a sufficient education to their students. We deal with the overload problem through our passion for ongoing and relentless learning, our focus on authentic problems, and our ability to confront chaos and complexity without fear.

At Apple, we treated new hires out of college as if they had no industrially useful education. We assumed they could read and write. That's all. The things they were taught in the universities barely touched the things that mattered to us. Kids in school were not learning about the latest software engineering ideas and were taught next to nothing about the latest technology. Their training wasn't practical, and their theoretical knowledge, if they remembered any of it from the lecture hall, was generally obsolete.

What this means for success is simple. *Knowledge workers succeed, not based on what they know, but rather how they learn.* It's the difference between a pantry and a supermarket. I don't stock my pantry with a year's supply of every kind of food. Even if I did, the food wouldn't be fresh. Instead, I go to the supermarket when I need something. The market has an amazing variety of anything I could want, whenever I want it. I keep myself from starving by living near a system that provides me with food, and by knowing how to use that system.

The supermarket of learning is online, a Google away. Or it's embodied in the minds of my colleagues, whom I email when I need emergency tutoring. It's in my personal pantry of books, two thousand of them, most of which I haven't read—they are standing by in case I need them.

All is learning fodder for buccaneers. We explore for ourselves. We may learn from a teacher or a formalized syllabus, but on our own terms and in our own time. We move between and among subjects without respect for disciplinary boundaries. We are skeptics who play with beliefs and try on philosophies. We create our own models of the world, or pluck from other thinkers as we see fit. We're responsible for our own errors.

"No prey, no pay" is the old buccaneering line. It dictates how I learn on the job. I ask myself what my clients need from me, I discover what I need to know to serve them well. My education follows necessity.

Not just immediate necessity. I also think ahead. How I can do my job better? I scout constantly, hunting for the next great secret, the next idea that transforms my work for the better. Ideas that may transform my industry.

PLAYING THE EXPERT GAME

Let me illustrate how this works with the example of my younger brother, Jon. After I dropped out of school I tried to convince him to do the same. But he didn't share my anger against the school system. He was content to walk the line other people had painted for him. He graduated and later earned a journalism degree at the University of Maine. He was editor of the school's daily newspaper there.

But by the time he finished his journalism degree, he had lost all interest in journalism as a profession.

He tried different things. He wrote a book, but writing for a living didn't appeal to him. He went the other direction and washed dishes at a country club. Have you ever heard of an ambitious dishwasher? He was one. Jon analyzed the dishwashing process, trying to maximize his efficiency. He studied the social dynamics, too, lecturing me about the tense politics among kitchen staff and wait staff.

He left that job and became a clerk at a bookstore. Once again he tried to understand the forces acting on his work; he tried to find new efficiencies. He looked for the fastest way to restock shelves or find a requested book. One of the things he noticed was that many customers came looking for books that had been featured on the *Oprah* show. He had an idea for making a special table just for Oprah books. His idea was rejected and he left that job, too. Ironically, within a year, *Oprah* displays had become commonplace in American bookstores.

He was frustrated in those jobs, because his ideas and ambition were not valued. So, I trained him to be a software tester. Jon was one of my first public students.

At first he didn't believe he could be a tester, because he had no training in computers. Like most people, lack of self-confidence is the first barrier to get over.

"You don't need computer training, Jonny, but you do need to start learning," I told him. "That's under your control. You can learn anything you want about computers, starting now."

I lectured him and I drilled him in the ways of examining technology to uncover its deficiencies. I stood him in front of a whiteboard and made him practice explaining his methods and results. Slowly he lost his fear.

I estimated it would take ten job interviews before someone was impressed enough with his presentation to hire him as an entry level tester. He did it in seven. Microsoft took him in.

He was successful there, too, as I had been at Apple. During his years at Microsoft he worked as a tester and test lead in three different groups. One day I visited him in his office, and he told me the secret of his success.

"I tried to take some of the classes they offer at Microsoft," he said, "But they don't help much. Most of them aren't directly related to my job."

"Yes, I find that, too. I don't have a lot of patience for classroom stuff."

"Then I tried collecting books."

On his desk, under the rubble of printouts and test data, I could see large squarish lumps that may have been books. There were also books heaped awkwardly onto nearby shelves.

"Cool." I fished one out of the pile. "*Advanced Developing with Excel 3.0 Macros?* Wait, this is obsolete."

"Yeah, I know, I scouted it out of a recycle bin. Don't roll your eyes, It could be useful in some way. Someday."

"Have you read these books?"

"Not really. I don't have time."

"Jon! You need to get with it, man."

"I have my *own* method."

"Okay, the classes don't help, and the books aren't helping, either. How do you learn your job? You lead a test team. Why does your boss think you know how to do that?"

"Well, I'm not an expert in anything, but my boss treats me as if I know exactly what to do. That's because when I need to do something, I know how to find someone around the building and ask for help. I learn from that guy, and later I pass that on to someone else. We all teach each other."

"Ah, you have a colleague network. A legion of super-friends. I do that, too! It's a polite little dance, isn't it?" I mused. "Sort of a game. We know there are gaps in our knowledge, but we are forgiven as long as we can get the job done. We do that by learning what we need to know, just in time. Or we do it by getting other people to help us. Or both."

"That's the Expert Game, brother. That's how we do it."

The Expert Game for Knowledge Workers

If . . .

- you are able to get important things done
- you are seen learning things on your own
- you are seen trying to do things even if you aren't sure how
- you share freely the things that you know
- you don't hide your ignorance, but also don't rest on it
- you honor what other people know
- you usually know how to find out what you don't yet know
- you know how to ask for help
- you offer to help people on their own terms

Then . . .

- no one cares whether you succeed by learning or by already knowing.
- no one minds if you mess up occasionally, because you learn from it.
- no one minds much if you don't know any given thing at any given time.
- you are treated as if you're smart and useful, even though you have much to learn.

Today Jon has gone buccaneer. He is also a testing consultant and trainer. People confuse him with me. We do crazy learning experiments together, such as reading ten books in one hour, or trying to find lessons about technical communication in a book on knitting.

11

Treasure Map

The power of a personal syllabus

Is it possible to gain a satisfying and respectable education if you only learn what you feel like learning? Yes! But how does that happen? Just as the original buccaneers navigated the deep blue sea, buccaneer-scholars can chart their own course on the great ocean of knowledge. They can attain an education without the guidance of an established institution.

The relentless scouting and the glorious feeling of being respected for my work drives my education ever outward. With each passing year, the expanding wavefront of knowledge and skill makes a rich, deep, and diversified education.

What I need to guide my education is a syllabus. A syllabus is the outline of things that I should learn. Since I rejected the syllabi of the schoolmasters, I needed to find one on my own. In buccaneering terms, I needed a treasure map. Among the first places I looked for one was the encyclopedia.

The Encyclopedia Is a Poor Syllabus

One comprehensive learning plan is to read the encyclopedia. That doesn't work for me.

I remember reading parts of the *Encyclopaedia Britannica* at the library when I was a kid. I believed that "reading the encyclopedia" would give me an education, but of course I had no patience for that. I mainly sat near the long shelf of its volumes and imagined reading them. When I grew up and got a credit card, my first purchase was a *Britannica* for my living room. The thirty volumes, standing ready on my bookshelf, seemed like an honor guard of knowledge. Again, I sat near them. I could see them while watching TV. But of course, all those millions of words in my home didn't change me in any important way. I was no more educated owning them than I had been visiting them at the library. Years later, when the entire *Encyclopaedia* became available on CD, I promptly purchased it. It was at my fingertips—I could look up any fact it contained in a few moments—yet still I didn't feel educated.

One day, it dawned on me. No matter how close I came to the facts of *Britannica,* my education would not change one little bit. Even if *Britannica* was somehow loaded into my brain, so that I could search it silently and instantly with my thoughts, I would still be the same man with the same education. I could win quiz games, sure, but I would not have any more power or perception or ability to solve authentic problems. I would not be better *educated.*

Memorizing a fact, or a million facts, doesn't change me and does little to help me unless I *digest* what I learn. I need to make sense of facts and see connections among them. I need to fit ideas into a schema that lets me put them to use. I need to brood and ponder.

I need to practice solving problems. I need to win knowledge, not just brush up against it. Then my consciousness will expand and I will become more powerful. That's what I mean by self-construction, otherwise known as education. Education is what we are, not what we can regurgitate.

With that realization, I lost interest in cramming the *entire Britannica* into my head.

An encyclopedia lays out human knowledge and orders it in a fashion that is meaningful and convenient to its authors. *Britannica* (and Wikipedia) is nice to have as a resource, but not as a syllabus. Someone else's way of ordering ideas is rarely the way my own mind is ready to take it in. I needed some principle or mechanism by which I could decide what to learn and when. I needed my *own* treasure map.

Scouting and the Syllabus

Here's how to create a syllabus. Step one, don't worry about a syllabus.

What I do: Instead of cramming and memorizing from an approved corpus of knowledge, I scout. I scout constantly. I haunt bookstores and libraries, the Web, and Amazon.com, looking for anything that might help. Friends send me links. I read blogs about science and history. When I scout, I scan immense stacks of material. I let the ideas boil in my mind for a little while and let them go. I make myself drunk with text and pictures. I don't even try to keep it all down. I binge and purge. I obsess and forget.

Then my syllabus appears bit by bit. It grows organically in a process much like *diffusion-limited aggregation*. (Do not be intimidated by that term! I only just discovered it myself while playing with physics simulation software I found on the Web. Go look it up in Wikipedia and see the beautiful pictures. See how simple the idea is? An orderly crystal can be produced from randomly moving molecules.) Here's how it works: As I live and learn, I stumble into some idea or technique that may help me solve an authentic problem. Learning about that idea leads me to more ideas as I ask myself questions:

- What are examples of this idea?
- How might this idea help me?
- Are there other ideas like this one?
- Where do I go to study this idea in detail?
- How can I practice this idea, right now?

Questions like these are like little magnets that attract yet more ideas. I apply the same questions to each new fact, concept, or object as I study.

After a while I begin to perceive a pattern in the ideas that I recently found useful or interesting. Often the patterns come with labels, such as "cognitive psychology" or "situated action theory." Sometimes I invent my own labels. Once in a while, I stop stumbling and write or draw an outline of the patterns and how they connect to each other—my syllabus. That lets me to scout with more efficiency and purpose.

This is another example of alternation. I accumulate ideas through open scouting, then I make sense of those differing ideas by drawing connections between them in my syllabus; then I go back to scouting.

EXAMPLE: THE UNIVERSE IN A GRAIN OF TESTING

When I was a kid, I wanted to be a physicist or a chemist. Perhaps a paleontologist. I needed adventure. I had never heard of software testing and I'm sure I would not have wanted to do that for a living. Playing with computer programs and noticing when they do something wrong? Where's the adventure in that? Sounds like a strange little job.

But the more I learned about testing, the bigger the job became to me. While some problems in products are obvious and easy to spot, most aren't. Some problems are invisible except under bizarre conditions. Products can do thousands of different things in millions of different variations, and I have time to check only a fraction of those possibilities. Which ones should I try? As I learned testing, it transformed from an easy task into a challenging puzzle. I began to feel like a hunter. I felt I was gliding silently down hyper-dimensional alleyways of logic, stalking electronic prey. Something like a virtual Batman. That's adventure!

As my view of the testing field expanded, I found that it touched upon many aspects of human experience. Testing is a tiny field, but it was like a keyhole through which I could see the whole world of knowledge. Here are some examples:

- **To test, we must move with confidence through a complex and confusing world.** We don't allow it to intimidate us. Therefore, we must be good at reading, observing, and drawing inferences about what we observe. We need to know how to work with formal and informal descriptions of products, and we need a big imagination about what could go wrong with them. We must rapidly analyze the products and situations we are presented with. We must see the product we are testing, as well as the context in which it will be used. *That means testing has much in common with science.*

- **To test is to cast light into the darkness, dispel illusions, and drive away ignorance.** Testing is a way of learning. It's also a way of *unlearning* things that aren't so. A tester is someone who knows that things could be different—different than they seem, different tomorrow than they are today, different over there than they are here. Therefore we must understand how people form beliefs about the world, so we can help anticipate and correct errors in those beliefs. We must look within ourselves to see our own biases and illusions, as well. This is an ever-branching process of questioning. *To use a fancy word, testing requires an understanding of epistemology (the study of how we come to know what we know).*

- **To test is to evaluate the risk.** We testers may not find every problem in a product, but we need to find the *bad* ones. Therefore we must understand what makes one problem worse than another, and what kinds of problems are more likely to occur. *This relates to engineering, but also to economics and human values and emotions.*

- **To test is to help our clients make better decisions through having a better understanding of the world.** Therefore we must know how to listen, negotiate, and explain the things that matter. We must understand how decisions are made in organizations. Because we will never have enough time to do a perfect job, we must know how to tell when our testing is good enough, and we must learn how to get the resources we need to do the work. *This requires business and social skills.*

GREAT SECRET

*Anything I learn
is a gateway
to everything else
I will ever know.*

I didn't go to school to discover the connections between testing and other fields. Most of it I didn't find even in books about testing. I simply approached my craft with a buccaneering attitude. I scouted, I struggled with authentic problems each day, I procrastinated, I plunged in, I incorporated each of the eleven elements and heuristics of buccaneering into my process. As a result, a specific career path (the field of testing) unfolded before me. One will unfold before you, too. I reinvented testing for myself, and made myself into a unique brand name among testers. Any buccaneer can do this in any chosen field.

Sometimes other testers find my syllabus a little crazy. Some of my rivals think that the things I study have nothing to do with testing. I half hope they continue to think that way, so that I can continue to find new solutions to problems they can't solve at all. But I also get excited when I meet a colleague who follows a different syllabus, because then I can plunder his ideas about what to study. I may discover an important blind spot in my own education.

Here is my syllabus for software testing as of this writing:

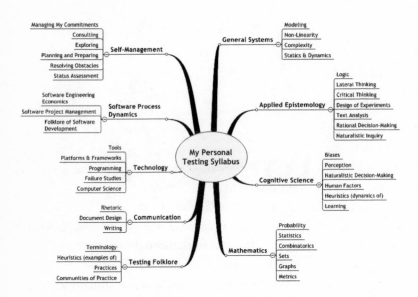

I made this tree by watching myself think about software testing and noticing the patterns of my scouting. Then I carried it around to colleagues and added to it based on their suggestions. I am not an expert in most of these areas. I'm an expert tester in that I have a working knowledge of each leaf on this tree, and I can bring that knowledge to bear to solve difficult and important problems.

Testing seems to lead to many other fields, and many other fields lead to testing. Today I see all of life from a testing point of view. Testing is a core part of my identity. It's no longer a strange little job. But then again, I bet that can be true for every other field, too. Call it the *Principle of Connection*. All seas are part of one great sea. Therefore, one way to find your syllabus for a powerful and general education is to begin with one thing you love to do, then let the nature of connected learning take its course.

EXAMPLE: A SYLLABUS OF QUESTIONS

In 1990 I decided to try something new: I hired a history tutor. Well, I hired Professor Aaron Goldman from San Jose State University and asked him to tutor me. I was expecting him to tell me what I should study. Instead he surprised me by asking what I wanted to do.

I had one immediate answer. "I have a book called *A Study of History*, by Arnold Toynbee. It's big, like a coffee table book, but with a whole lot of dense text. I want to work through that."

"That's sounds like a good idea," he said. "But do you have a more general goal? What attracts you to the study of history?"

That got me thinking about my syllabus. I went away for a while to work it out. What came to me were questions. My syllabus became organized around those questions.

Questions are lovely things. They are dynamic. They are rich in implications. Questions lead to more questions. They bring thoughts to life. I love the flexibility of a syllabus formed from questions, and it worked well for studying history.

Thumbnail Learning Goals
for James Bach

My basic goal is to learn more about my own nature by studying humanity in general. History, mythology, philosophy and psychology are the fields that I think will cover my needs, in addition to a broad reading of world literature.

Second priorities are geography, economics, finance and sociology.

By the year 2000 I'd like to have a well rounded working knowledge of all of these fields sufficient to support my "life's work".

A more immediate goal for history study is that I want to have reasonably clear and supportable opinions based in history about the following questions:

What is human nature?
How is male nature different from female?
What are the general patterns of history?
How do wars start?
How do great ideas spread? How do they die out?
What mistakes does mankind keep making?
What progress has mankind made?
How do civilizations develop and why do they fall?
What are the roots of American society?
How have economies developed through the ages?

Also,

Is there a discipline to historical study?
Are there different kinds of histories?
How do I make a historical analysis?
How do I tell a good historical analysis from a poor one?

The kinds of knowledge I need from a tutor are:

-   **The components of a complete education in History**
-   **A reading path to attain that education**

and then from time to time,

-   **An assessment of where I stand on the path**

174

Look at my questions. Notice I don't care much about dates, countries, or great men and women of the past. Instead, my questions relate to structures and dynamics in history. Yes, the Roman Empire fell on some date. What was it? 476? That is not interesting history to me. I care about *why* Rome fell, not whether it fell on a Tuesday.

What authentic problem motivated my questions? My need to make sense of the world. I wanted to understand human events on a millennial global scale, as well as a household daily scale. At the time, I thought that having the ability to analyze society and history in terms of the questions on my syllabus would help me be more comfortable even within the confines of my own life experience. Eighteen years later, I feel that the strategy worked. I obsessed over history for four months or so in 1990, then forgot about it. I return periodically to ask the same questions again, and so refresh and deepen my feel for human society.

The syllabus helped me in another way. Back then, I was still nervous about learning from other people, especially *teachers*. I was still angry about how I was treated in the school system. Hiring my own teacher helped, and the syllabus was a way to negotiate the terms of the tutoring.

Overall, my experience has led me to the conviction that there are no educational problems, suffered before the age of twenty, that cannot easily be fixed later in life. I suspected this was true when I was twenty-one. It was at that age I decided to become an expert software tester. Today I am almost exactly double that age. Now I know.

12

Dr. Bach

Buccaneering in the long run

What has come of my buccaneering, thirty years since my elementary school rebellion?

> *Dear Dr. Bach:*
>
> *On behalf of Phil Laplante and Editor Jeff Voas, I cordially invite you to contribute an entry on "Testing a Service" for the forthcoming Encyclopedia of Software Engineering. . . .*
>
> *Dear Dr. Bach:*
>
> *We wanted to express our gratitude to you, on behalf of National Science Foundation and the scientific and engineering communities, for your participation in NSF's*

merit review process, considered by many to be the "gold standard" of peer review. . . .

Dear Dr. Bach:

I invite you to review the above referenced manuscript submitted to IEEE Software. The abstract appears at the end of this letter. Please let me know within 3 days if you will be able to participate in the review process. If you are unable to review at this time, I would appreciate your recommending another expert reviewer. . . .

—actual emails I received

I haven't gone back to school. I still don't have a PhD or anything else. But I do occasionally receive emails from academics who know me only by reputation. Often they assume I *must* have a doctorate. In the academic world, you can't achieve a position of respect and authority without one.

I'm not well known among academics, because I don't publish in academic journals. But provocative ideas travel far. Some professors pay attention to trends in industry, and some of my work is assigned reading in university courses, such as those at MIT and Stanford.

My broader reputation in the computing field emerged when I took ideas grounded in the authentic problems of my daily work and shared them publicly. At first I was just trying to contribute to the craft and improve my portfolio. But going public soon turned into a key element of my education.

177

Hoisting the Black Flag

I started by attending local meetings of software testers and teaching a few introductory classes at employment agencies for potential new testers. In that way, I caught the notice of a company called Borland International, which recruited me to run a test team for them. Borland valued my experience at Apple, appreciated my technical knowledge, and didn't seem to care about my lack of schooling. This made sense because Borland was founded by Philippe Kahn, a maverick who favored independent thinkers. The slogan at Borland was, "We are barbarians!" Black pirate flags hung here and there around the campus. They were a hungry, competitive, and adventurous culture. I loved working there.

I learned a lot at Borland, where I was encouraged to try as many new ideas as possible. We were constantly experimenting and looking for better ways to work. As my confidence grew, I wanted to share my ideas more widely. So, in 1993 I applied to present at an international testing conference in Washington, DC.

Here's how conferences work in my world: There are academic conferences and practitioner conferences. Academic conferences focus on people with acceptable academic credentials who do obscure studies in laboratories. Most of those academic results appear irrelevant or unworkable to practitioners who must produce technology on a deadline, for paying customers. In some industries, I bet there's a strong partnership between academics and practitioners. Not in the software field. In the software field, being nonacademic could make me more likely to be taken seriously.

I picked a topic the opposite of anything I'd ever read or heard from a theorist. My talk was about how all the textbooks of testing were wrong. They declared that testing must be carefully and meticulously planned *in advance* or else it will fail, yet when I looked around my company, most testing was nothing like that. Most high-impact software testing I had seen was improvised in the moment—and still it worked. I would explain why unplanned testing was *better*.

It was the same attitude toward work as I'd always had to my schooling: promoting solutions to authentic problems while opposing hollow traditions.

When the conference organizers accepted my proposal, I was a bit shocked and a bit awed. I even bought a suit. My first suit. That's how freaked out I was. Technical guys in Silicon Valley don't wear suits.

When I got to the conference, I rushed to the registration booth to collect my speaker badge. It came with a special ribbon. I wanted to pin the ribbon on my suit and strut around the lobby in full ceremonial dress.

As I stepped up to register, someone tapped my shoulder. It was Boris Beizer, the best-known author in the testing field. I had been reading his books since my first week at Apple. His books were full of advice. Most of it didn't work for me.

GREAT SECRET

*Buccaneering is audacious.
Even the friendliest buccaneers
frighten the authorities.*

The man was true to his writing.

"I have a *bone* to pick with you!" he cried.

"Boris Beizer! Wow, good to meet you, sir. What can I do for you?"

"I wanted to talk to you about your presentation. I'm on the program committee, you know. I voted in favor of your talk."

"Thank you, I'm glad to be here."

"It's bullshit, you know. Your talk? It's bullshit. I want to be clear on that."

Ah, debate! Buccaneers love a good debate. We argued for ninety minutes. The staff shooed us away from the desk, because our loud voices were disrupting registration. It seemed to me that Beizer was trying to establish his dominance. He wanted me to recognize him as the alpha test consultant. I was determined to hold my own.

Boris explained that he voted for my presentation in the spirit of diversity, but that he thought I was obviously ignorant about the craft of software testing. I countered that the methods I promoted were popular in the Valley simply because they worked. They were popular at Microsoft, too, and were an important part of the company's flexible approach that allowed them to soar above the rest of the industry. He replied that Microsoft's terrible methods would drive them out of business within five years (this was in 1993). (He later denied saying that during our conversation, but I clearly recall it.)

It went on like that. Back and forth.

By the time he stomped off, I was depressed. Not because Beizer didn't appreciate my ideas. I'm used to that. Honest debate would sort that out. What depressed me was hearing that he controlled whether I would ever again be allowed to speak at a major conference. Perhaps he and his graybeard friends could put an end to my ambition.

Up till then, I enjoyed the testing field, because it was free and open. In buccaneering terms, I sailed where I pleased. There was no "naval authority" to tell me what I could and couldn't do. Now I felt as if I'd met one of the admirals, and the admiral was not amused. I had graduated from petty raider to public menace.

I gave my little talk the next day, expecting to be booed. I was ready for an audience of old men with goatees and pince-nez glasses, waving their canes, throwing down their top hats, yelling things like "What a preposterous foolery!"

How surprising that the audience applauded, instead. Outside the lecture room I was immediately surrounded by practicing testers who wanted to talk to me about their own experiences with improvised software testing. "Finally someone telling it like it is. Why don't more speakers have common sense?"

When I got home, invitations to speak at other conferences soon followed. Word spread about the crazy kid who challenged Beizer.

I'd stumbled into a market that the graybeards were not serving. Maybe sometimes it takes a Blackbeard to get the job done. I had stormed and captured my first prize.

A Society of Buccaneers

Reputation can be self-inflating—I found myself struggling to keep up with the things that strangers told each other about me. I felt pressure to become as knowledgeable and skillful as people *assumed* I was. The fear of being exposed as uneducated in front of a large audience of critical thinkers drove me to prepare thoroughly for each conference and speaking engagement. I like that kind of pressure.

I joined every professional organization I could join. I read all the software journals.

I still saw myself as a solitary outlaw doomed to scandalize and titillate the lawful citizens of the craft. I wanted to be on a team, to be needed, but I wanted to make my own independent contribution. When I was forced to collaborate more closely, it often turned into a struggle for dominance.

In 1995 I took on a new job as chief scientist at STLabs, a software testing company. This gave me a budget to buy books and travel to conferences. Most of my job was studying; the rest was teaching. For a few years it was a heavenly opportunity. It was the perfect job for me.

My new freedom as a company-sponsored buccaneer-scholar gave me the opportunity to meet many new colleagues from all over the industry. Two of these would transform how I saw my work and my education: Gerald M. Weinberg and Cem Kaner.

Jerry Weinberg is an eminent figure in the world of computing. He was a member of the team that created the very first computer operating system (think: the first Windows, except without any windows). He was the architect on the project that formed the very first test team, in 1958. He first published his ideas on testing in 1961. Jerry nearly dropped out of high school, same as me.

"I didn't drop out," Jerry told me. "Though I cut virtually all of my classes in high school, I did come to an agreement with the school authorities that they would graduate me if I didn't bother the other students and encourage them to cut and do buccaneering learning." He went to college *after* he joined IBM, eventually earning a doctorate. There was some awkwardness while he was getting his undergraduate degree, apart from dropping out of college twice—

the textbook for one of his classes turned out to be one Jerry himself had written.

He was the first person I'd met in my life who inspired me to say, "If I study hard for thirty years, maybe I can be like him." His specialty is general systems thinking and psychology for technical workers. He taught me about the human dynamics of technical work. From him I learned how to take criticism, and how to contribute to a team without trying to control it. I first learned about heuristics from Jerry. He taught me about Follow the Energy.

Jerry gave me precious advice on writing, procrastinating, and succeeding as a consultant. He taught me how to let go of stress about getting things done. He turned one of his lectures to me about writing into a book, *Weinberg on Writing: The Fieldstone Method*.

Basically, Jerry taught me how to be an *adult*. To fully explain what that means would take another book. Fortunately he has already written dozens of them. I recommend them all.

Cem Kaner (his first name is pronounced "kem") taught me how to be a professional intellectual. Cem has a doctorate in psychology and a law degree, as well. He's one of the most systematically educated people I know, and yet one of the most humble about what he knows. His studies are deep and his papers are heavily footnoted. Cem inspired me to study the philosophy and ethics of science.

In 1997, Cem introduced a new tradition to our community: the *peer conference*. A peer conference is something like a round table discussion. Each member of the audience is also a speaker. Speakers present stories from their own lives, rather than abstract concepts. Most importantly, anyone who speaks is required to stand and answer questions and challenges. Peer conferences foster *contrasting ideas*.

I'd like to pass along some of the heuristics I learned from Cem about exchanging and criticizing ideas. These heuristics have become a sort of moral code among my closest colleagues, and I think they apply to any buccaneering community.

Criticize the Best Example

I like to fight bullies. Twenty years ago, in my industry, one of those bullies was called "Total Quality Management." It struck me as a philosophy of using simplistic diagrams and buzz phrases to try to improve quality, while accusing dissenters of "resisting change." I hadn't met a TQM promoter whom I respected. But as I wrote and spoke against TQM, Cem stopped me and asked whether I had read the original material on TQM. I hadn't. I was making all my judgments based on copycat consultants. Cem shook his head. "James, when you criticize bad examples of an idea, your criticism applies only to the bad examples. Read the original thinkers on TQM. Find the best examples and criticize those. Then your arguments will be more powerful, *and* people will take you more seriously."

Sympathetic Criticism First

I don't like the idea of constructive criticism, at least not the way I was taught it. Constructive criticism, I'm told, means that you say something nice about the heap of junk before you point out that it's a heap of junk. Intellectually I can understand the value of saying that, but I feel like I'm being patronizing. Sympathetic criticism is different. To criticize sympathetically is to judge something on its own terms. I try to imagine the context and the spirit in which the idea or product was created. I appreciate the problems it was trying to solve. Then I criticize it from that point of view. I do that before I attack the idea from my own point of view. Cem once lectured me for two hours because I criticized another colleague unsympathetically.

Knives in the Chest, Not in the Back

If I'm going to fight someone, I come at them in the open. They know who I am, and they know I'm fighting them. This rule sometimes takes a lot of courage. If it weren't for the respect I crave from my friends, I might not have the strength to follow it.

Integrity is a Struggle, Not a Badge

In one of the companies I worked for, just after I joined, I asked in a meeting what people did to develop their expertise. There was an uncomfortable silence. I asked again. Then one fellow spoke up, rather irritated. "James, these are the finest people I've ever worked with. How dare you imply that they aren't expert enough?" I was surprised to hear this, since I have to work hard to maintain my own competence. Integrity is like that, too. Integrity has little meaning except in situations where we are tempted to sidestep the truth, or skip a process that we know we should honor. Integrity is a constant struggle. I didn't think much about it until I witnessed the way Cem worked at it when we first met. He would brood about conflicts of interest in his own career and ask my opinion. At first I was bemused. He was so serious about what seemed like tiny matters to me. Then I became embarrassed, because I *wasn't* brooding about those things. Over time, to earn Cem's respect, my standards rose, and I found myself struggling for integrity, too.

Many people—I used to be one—think of integrity as the natural consequence of good intentions. "I must have integrity because I feel like a good person." But that's not enough. Integrity means living consistently with how you present yourself to others. This is hard because my natural human condition seems to be self-contradiction and self-centeredness. I've discovered that I unconsciously lie to myself, sometimes. I find it easy to flatter someone powerful, even if I believe them a fool. I find it easy to support an idea just because my friends ask me to. I try to do the difficult thing and maintain my integrity, but I don't always succeed. I hope to be forgiven for my lapses, as I try to forgive others.

For buccaneers, it's a mixed issue. On one hand, we often don't live by other people's values. We can be rogues in more ways than one. We experiment with breaking rules. On the other hand, we buccaneers want good reputations so people will cooperate with us (it's so much easier when the merchant vessels surrender without a fight). We also may find it easier to tell the unvarnished truth as we see it, because we are more comfortable offending people (as long as they're the right people to offend).

I learned long ago to hate the sick feeling in my stomach when I tell a lie and the similar sick feeling of losing the respect of a friend. This makes integrity an authentic problem for me.

Cem taught me that integrity is not something you can just declare. Let me demonstrate: *I have integrity!* See what I mean? What are you thinking? You're probably thinking something like, "What a sanctimonious jerk! Why is he making a big deal about this? Yeah, right, integrity. Give me a break!" Am I right?

The reputation for integrity, I've found, is earned over a long period of time. It's what other people who've worked with you say about you. Integrity is an ongoing struggle, because once lost—once I take the easy route to a big score—it's very hard to get it back again.

You might say Jerry helped me relax my expectations for myself so that I could live with less stress and worry, while Cem helped me raise my aspirations so I could live with a greater sense of purpose. Both of them are community builders who showed me the value of running with a pack, and demonstrated how that's different from being stuck in a herd.

GREAT SECRET

*To be a part of
a buccaneering community is to be
challenged, debated, and irritated
by your most loyal friends.*

HUNTING IN PACKS

A pack is a cooperative group of hunters. Each member of the community shows personal initiative, independent judgment, and critical thinking. With my pack mentality, I cultivate friends I respect and trust, and listen to them, without being dominated by them. The organizing principle of a herd is fear. It is a defensive community. The most important thing about being in a herd is not to disrupt the order.

A herd sees itself as surrounded by danger. A pack sees itself as surrounded by opportunities: prey.

A typical public school in the United States is all about honoring the herd. The students are supposed to be sheep, but too many of the teachers are just older and fatter sheep. Schoolism is a herd mentality.

Public schools could work in a more personal way, were it not for the money, parental fear, and the corporate and political interests that pollute the system. A school system could trust students to learn and support them in their learning. If they don't want to learn, let them leave. If they change their minds, let them return. No big deal. Two systems already do it that way: public libraries and the Internet.

The herd mentality is not restricted to schools. It's all over the place. It suffuses my little industry, for sure. We all value decorum and merit in the exchange of ideas. But under pressure, it's often not easy to have both at once. As I began to meet and debate with the many consultants, authors, and speakers in my field, I discovered that they came in two broad categories: people who value decorum over merit, and people who value merit over decorum. The first group is much larger.

The top priority in my industry—for the many people who go to conferences—is for there to be no arguing. The experts should simply agree and move on. Many people go to conferences in order to find the One Right Answer to their questions. Many so-called experts go along with this culture, because it means easy money from consulting contracts.

Once, for a short time, I worked in a large consulting firm. For them, "pleasing the customer" was the most important thing. But the truth wasn't always pleasing. There was a lot of pressure on me to get billable hours and to toe the company line even if I disagreed with it.

I couldn't stand it. I like being with the other kind of consultant. The critical thinker. The complainer. The one who reinvents wheels, rethinks the obvious, struggles to get it right instead of just sounding right. The one who appreciates the messiness of practical life. The buccaneer.

I want to be around buccaneers. One example is my friend Michael Butler. Michael seems to dabble in everything. Michael called me at 10 p.m. recently because he was excited about his discovery that the ancient Greeks had two words for "time." He went on for a while about Isocrates, a Greek orator I'd never heard of. We discussed black swans, the ludic fallacy, and proper soldering technique. Michael's thoughts warm me like a campfire.

Some buccaneers barely support themselves. I'm thinking of the limo driver who revealed to me that he is also a trained analytical philosopher who sings opera and builds handcrafted wooden boats. All that, and he's about to go on welfare. It is not easy to reconcile an independent mind with the need to make a living.

But there are others who are fabulously prosperous, like inventor and author Simon Quellen Field. Simon worked with me at Borland. We used to have friendly debates about the value of scientific method. His desk was always covered with little mechanical and electric gadgets he created for fun. Simon is the classic Silicon Valley success story. Last I heard he worked at Google, but he no longer needs to work at all.

Remember, a successful buccaneer is not necessarily one who is wealthy in conventional terms. Success for a buccaneer means being joyfully engaged in the lifelong project of making a better self. For a lot of us it also means making a better community, too. We feel engaged when we exceed our own expectations and are reaching toward aspirations that challenge us. For aspiring buccaneers, coming to terms with expectations and aspirations is critical. The ugly-duckling syndrome is common among younger buccaneers who still imagine that they should fit in with landlubbers instead of exploring the deep blue.

I love being around other buccaneers. We spur each other on. We trade great secrets. With our pack mentality we support each other without demanding blind conformity. We gain the power of community without losing our individual identities to it.

The importance of colleagues was the last big piece of the puzzle, for me. By the turn of the millennium, my education gained new energy and depth. I was running my own little business, and keeping a steady pace of innovation in collaboration with my buccaneer companions. My first book, written as a collaboration with two friends, became a bestseller in the software testing world.

In my work, I can afford to live with passion and integrity. I speak my mind openly, and I insist on doing my best work for my clients. Yes, more companies would hire me if I would bend a little and just tell them what they want to hear. That's okay. I don't need more. With the whole world as my market, there are plenty of people out there who want the services I offer. Other buccaneers recognize who I am. That's good enough for me.

I have my sails set and the wind is fresh. I hope to see you on the open sea.

Epilogue

At the helm

August 13, 2007. "Which is the jib halyard, and which is the spinnaker halyard?" asked Captain Ben, as his 26-foot sailing yacht rocked beneath us.

From my point of view on the bow, the two lines looked identical. Both lines curved down from pulleys at the top of the mast.

"I don't know." I replied.

"Well, logically, which should it be?"

"They're the same. I don't see any distinction."

"Look more closely."

Captain Ben runs a yachting school out of Rosario Marina. Long ago he was an elementary schoolteacher and then a motorcycle racer. The racing part may account for the steely glint in his eyes and the schoolteacher part for their twinkle. I like that combination. He's the perfect instructor for me, pushing me a bit beyond what I think I should be doing.

"What do you think?" he prompted.

"Okay . . . Hmm. On closer examination they are identical."

"No, they are *not*. This line goes to the *outside* pulley. The spinnaker sail is outside of the jib sail; therefore this must be the spinnaker halyard."

"There's only a three-inch difference between those pulleys! Does it really matter?"

"It matters. That difference is enough to foul the lines. You'll see what I mean when you hoist the spinnaker, later on. Now come down here and tell me what's wrong with the mainsheet rigging."

I got out my Moleskine notebook and wrote, "*A critical part of learning new skill: learning distinctions . . . distinctions invisible to untrained eye. . . .*" I underlined "distinctions" a few times. I carry my Moleskine everywhere. My Sharpie calligraphy pen, too. Every useful thought goes in the notebook. One out of fifty pays off, and sometimes they pay off big.

"What are you doing?" asked the Captain.

I wrote, "*A pattern of distinctions? . . . distinction matrix? . . . contradistinctions? Ben tests for distinctions BEFORE explaining them. Dialectical distinction construction?*"

"I might have to put you in my book, Ben," I said as I jammed the notebook back into my waterproof vest. "I'm getting a lot of ideas, here."

Sailing was part of my work that day. Research, I told myself. Also procrastination, since I'd made a bold boast that I would have a new chapter by the end of the week. Here I was, sailing. It's what I felt like doing, so it had to be part of the writing.

The Captain reminded me that the jib sheet must first pass through the turning block. It was easy to fix.

Everything is a part of it. Always. My education is my reaction to whatever happens. I develop ideas, I write, I teach. This is my life.

"Wait a sec, Captain." I fished out my notebook and wrote, *"Zero-point learning? Like zero-point energy. Seems to come from nowhere. Realizing what already is learned, that I didn't know I knew."*

He raised the mainsail. It pivoted into the wind and fluttered innocently.

"Time to go, James," called Captain Ben. "Take the helm. There's a west wind over the point. You won't need the motor."

He leapt off the boat and shoved it clear of the dock, me with it. "Helm, please."

"I'm going solo?" We hadn't discussed this.

"Happy sailing, James."

At the helm, notebook stowed. I hauled in on the mainsheet. The wind kissed the sail and the fluttering ended. The sails powered up. The boat leaned a bit, as if gathering its thoughts. Then we surged forward.

James and Captain Ben return from a lesson.
(photo by Lenore Bach)

193

Acknowledgments

This book would not have been written if my father, Richard Bach, hadn't asked me to write it in 1982, and then again in 1983, '84, '85, and every year until 2007. It couldn't have been written without the extreme patience and encouragement of my wife, Lenore, who provided me the space and time to write. I am also grateful to my friends and family who helped do the heavy editing on the book, especially in its early stages: Richard Bach, Lenore Bach, Jonathan Bach, Laura Saba, and Whitney Frick at Scribner.

Thank you to my agents Jim Levine and Dan Greenberg, who showed me how this is more than just a book.

Many others commented on the manuscript in ways that caused me to improve it, including: Jerry Weinberg, Chris Morgan, Michael Bolton, Sabryna Bach, Cem Kaner, Becky Fiedler, Jonathan Kohl, Jackie Meyer, Michelle Schroeder, Ben Simo, Stani Vlasseva, Marina Michaels, Julian Harty, Ben Walther, Bernie Berger, Adam Goucher, Pradeep Soundararajan, Shrini Kulkarni, and Karen Johnson.

Finally, I'm grateful for my son Oliver, who has surpassed me by dropping out of seventh grade.